·COUNTRY PATTERNS

A Sampler of Nineteenth Century
Rural Homes and Gardens

1841-1883

·Edited by Donald J. Berg·

ANTIQUITY REPRINTS, BOX 370, ROCKVILLE CENTRE, NY 11571

Calvert Vaux, VILLAS AND COTTAGES, 1857

DESIGN FOR STABLE, ETC.

Index

WELL-HOUSE.

George E. & F.W. Woodward, ARCHITECTURE, LANDSCAPE GARDENING AND RURAL ART, 1867

A BIRD-HOUSE.

CHICKEN-COOP.

Foreword

In the nineteenth century "Country" was a style as well as a place, just as it is today. Americans who lived on farms, in rural villages, or who escaped the city to vacation homes realized the beauty of the simple country life. In their homes, furnishings, garden buildings and landscaping, they sought practical, honest designs that harmonized with the natural setting and contrasted drastically with the more elaborate Victorian styles of the bustling cities.

This new book presents a small sampling of yesterday's country design, selected from nineteenth century architectural "Pattern" books and mail-order catalogs as well as from "Home and Garden" features in popular magazines.

ABOUT THIS BOOK

The material in this volume is reprinted directly from books and magazines originally published between 1841 and 1883. We hope that you will excuse the variations in type and the imperfections in printing that result when reproductions are made of time-worn pages directly from the pages themselves. The titles of each of the pages have been reset for this book, but they are in the exact words of the originals. Each design or feature article is credited to its architect or author; the book or magazine from which it was reproduced; and the earliest year of publication.

Copyright 1982
Printed in the U.S.A.

Library of Congress
Catalog Card No.: 82-70255
Berg, Donald
COUNTRY PATTERNS
Rockville Centre, N.Y.
Antiquity Reprints
80p.
8204   820119
I.S.B.N. 0-937214-05-1

An Irregular Country House

Samuel Sloan, HOMESTEAD ARCHITECTURE, 1861

IRREGULAR in plan and general outline, yet neat and chaste in detail, the design before us is a fair type of the beauty that may be attained without a tendency to extravagance in the exterior adornment of an edifice springing from an irregular basis.

ACCOMMODATION.—By a reference to fig. 2 , the plan of first floor, the internal arrangements will be perceived almost at a glance. A through hall B is entered from the piazza A. This hall contains the stairs, and affords access, by a side passage, to the kitchen E. The parlor C is 15 by 30 feet, and has a rectangular bay-window, communicating by a lengthened window with the veranda I. The dining-room D has also a bay-window, seen in the perspective view, which, by the way, is reversed from the plan. F is the butler's pantry, G a wood-shed, and H a kitchen closet.

The plan of the second floor exhibits the arrangement of the chambers. K is the landing of the stairs in the front building, from which the three chambers L are entered, and from which also the stairs are continued to the roof-story, in which three very comfortable bed-rooms may be fitted up.

A passage from the half-landing of the stairs leads to the bath-room M and the adjoining bed-room N, over the kitchen.

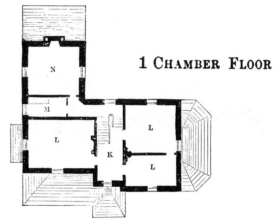

1 CHAMBER FLOOR

This house could be very efficiently warmed by a single furnace, the proximity of the flues being quite favorable to that mode: the hall, parlor, and dining-room, and the three chambers over, could all be kept comfortably warm, as the central position of the flues involves but little loss of heat.

CONSTRUCTION.—This design admits with equal facility the use of wood or more solid materials. The thickness of walls, as drawn, indicates the use of stone, which, in many districts, is the cheapest material. The pitch of the roof seems to demand shingle or slate; the drawing represents them of varied form.

ESTIMATE.—Built of stone and rough-cast in a neat, careful manner, and all the workmanship substantial and well finished, the cost of this house, in Pennsylvania or Ohio, will not vary much from $4600.

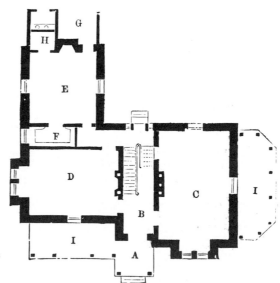

2

PRINCIPAL FLOOR.

Chamber Suite

CHAMBER SUITE No. 9.—From Warren Ward & Co.

This is a very stylish suite, after English designs, made both in Ash and Black-Walnut, and composed of the same pieces as No. 10. This is made with the Dressing-Case as illustrated (size of glass, 20x44), and with the French Bureau.

A.J. Bicknell, SPECIMEN BOOK OF ONE HUNDRED ARCHITECTURAL DESIGNS, 1878

Chamber Suite

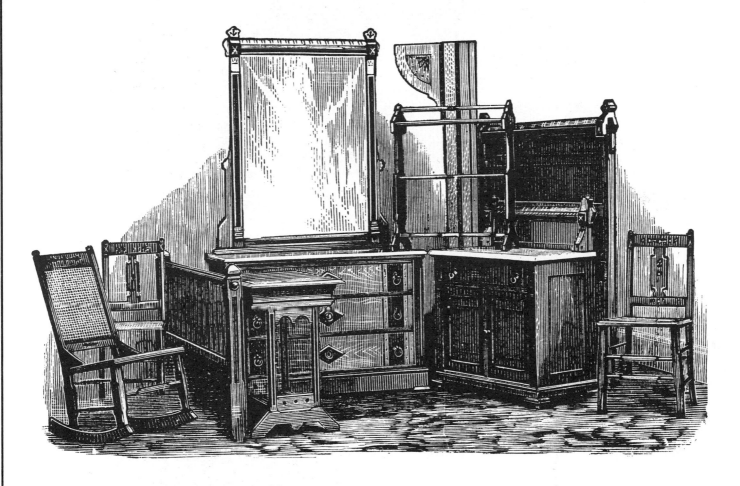

CHAMBER SUITE NO. 10.—From Warren Ward & Co.

This suite, made after Eastlake's designs, either in Ash or Black-Walnut, is very chaste and elegant, and is finished with either marble or wood tops. The pieces are : a Bedstead, French Dressing Bureau (French Plate Glass, 30 x 38), Washstand, Table, two Chairs, Rocker and Towel-Stand.

A.J. Bicknell, SPECIMEN BOOK OF ONE HUNDRED ARCHITECTURAL DESIGNS, 1878

George E. & F.W. Woodward, COUNTRY HOMES, 1865

Plan

Cottage Stable

STALL

II'6'X24

STALL CARRIAGE ROOM

16 X 20

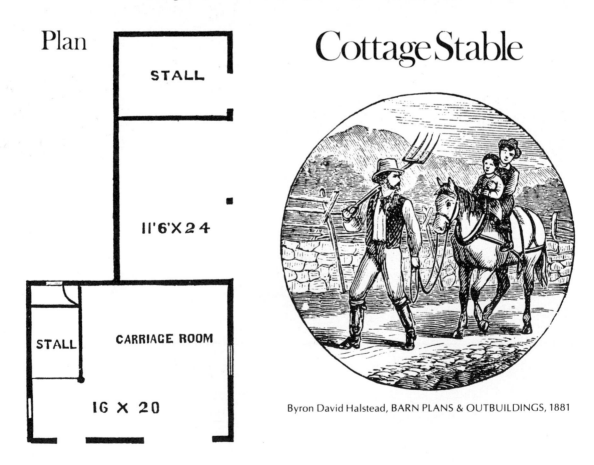

Byron David Halstead, BARN PLANS & OUTBUILDINGS, 1881

The vignette represents a study for a simple cottage, designed as a residence for men employed on the farm and in other operations about the estate. The cottage is in full view from the principal drive-road, and it therefore seemed worth while to consider it as an accessory in the landscape as well as a convenient home for those who were to live in it. The other side of the house showing the veranda would probably have offered a more picturesque view, but the vignette will serve to give a general idea of the simple effect aimed at. The basement, entered from a door on the outside, as shown on the sketch, was designed to be fitted up, for the use of the family, as a wash-room, and to be provided with drying-closet, ironing-room, etc. The principal floor explains itself, the two bedrooms below being for the housekeeper's use, and the chamber plan above, containing three roomy bedrooms, being set apart for the use of the men. Such a cottage, with the basement finished off, should cost about $1400 or $1500. In this instance the outlay was increased, from various causes, to $1800.

A Farm Cottage

Calvert Vaux, VILLAS AND COTTAGES, 1857

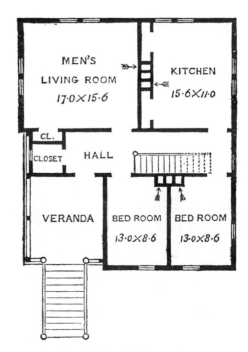

PLAN OF PRINCIPAL FLOOR.

CRANK HANDLE AND PORCELAIN KNOB.

PLAIN FACE LATCH.

ASTRAGAL FACE LATCH.

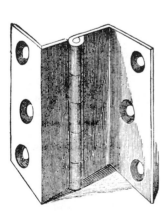

ESPAGNLETTE BOLT.

Cottage Hardware

The Baldwin & Many Co., New York

Gervase Wheeler, RURAL HOMES, 1851

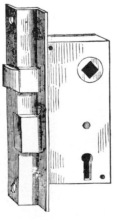

HAT AND COAT HOOK.

SILVER PLATED GOTHIC FRONT DOOR BELL-PULL.

BLIND OR DORMER WINDOW FASTENING.

FRENCH WINDOW HINGE.   RABBETED LOCK.

A.J. Downing & Calvert Vaux, VILLAS AND COTTAGES, 1857

A Symmetrical Country Home

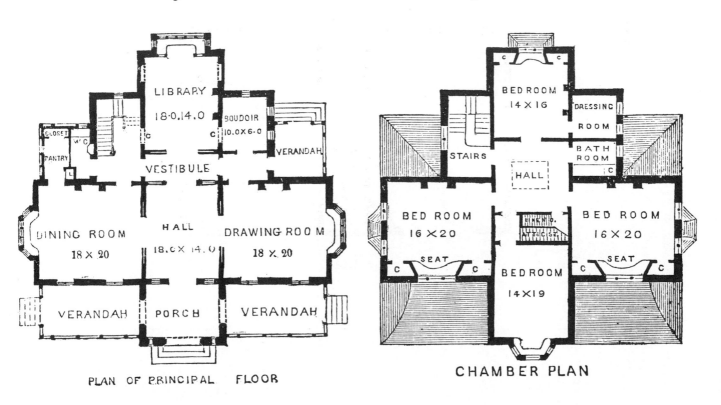

PLAN OF PRINCIPAL FLOOR

CHAMBER PLAN

Stable

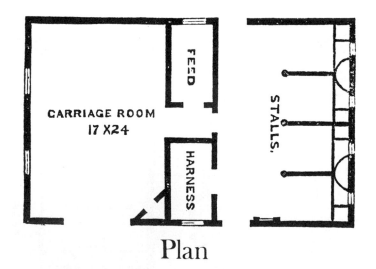

CARRIAGE ROOM
17 X24

FEED

HARNESS

STALLS.

Plan

George E. & F.W. Woodward, COUNTRY HOMES, 1865

Ice House

It is only within a few years that ice, in all seasons, has been classed among the necessaries of life. In large cities it is indispensable, but the cool spring-house or cellar in the country impresses many with the idea that ice, in summer months, can only be regarded as a luxury. Along with other conveniences in keeping with this progressive age, the ice-house has its place, and a country-seat of any pretensions is not complete without it.

It is simple in construction, and can be built very cheaply of rough materials, or made as elaborate as is desirable. It forms a pretty feature about the grounds, if treated with some architectural taste.

George E. & F.W. Woodward, COUNTRY HOMES, 1865

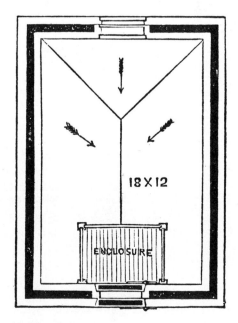

Plan

Cottage Furniture

GODEY'S LADY'S BOOK, 1849

In the designs for cottage furniture, we furnish the cheapest and prettiest articles that can be manufactured. We wish to convince our readers that they can at the same time, with the aid of the patterns we give, combine utility, beauty and economy.

Fig. 1. A DRESSER. The middle drawer, which is drawn out, has a lift-out box or tray,

Fig. 1.

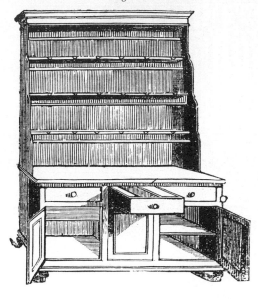

Fig. 2.

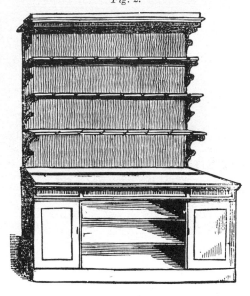

which is divided in the centre for knives, forks and spoons in daily use ; and underneath, in the bottom of the drawer, is a space for those not in use. The other two drawers are for clean table-cloths and towels. The cupboard in front is made in three panels, to look uniform ; but it has only two compartments, one for glasses and tea-cups and saucers, the other for fruits, sweet-meats, spices, &c.

Fig. 2. A dresser having beads on the edge to hold on the plates and dishes. The three drawers are for table-cloths, &c., as in *Fig.* 1, and the closets for corresponding purposes.

Fig. 3. A design for a sideboard in the Gothic style.

Fig. 4. The same open. The top compartment is for table-cloths, the others for table furniture.

Fig. 3.

Fig. 4.

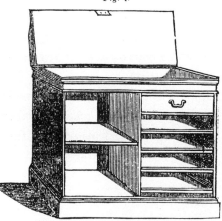

Cottage

H.W. Cleveland, William & Samuel D. Backus, VILLAGE AND FARM COTTAGES, 1856

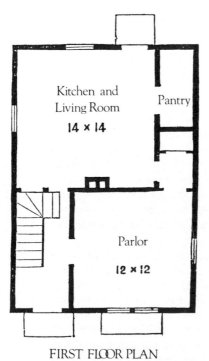

Kitchen and Living Room 14 × 14

Pantry

Parlor 12 × 12

FIRST FLOOR PLAN

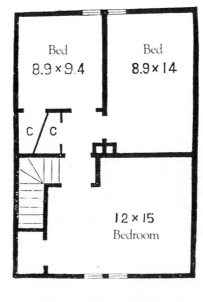

Bed 8.9 × 9.4

Bed 8.9 × 14

C C

12 × 15 Bedroom

SECOND FLOOR PLAN

A.J. Downing, THE HORTICULTURIST, 1846

VIEW OF A COMMON COUNTRY HOUSE. 1

Improving A Country Home

In *figure* 1, is seen a building that our readers will recognize at a glance, as the portrait of a plain country house, common in almost every neighborhood. Whilst there is perhaps nothing mean in the expression of this house, neither is there any thing in the least tasteful, or above the character of *common-place*. It belongs to the large class of dwellings whose presiding architectural genius is that of the "*bare and bald.*"

In *figure* 2, is seen our proposed alteration and improvement of this house.

In the first place, to give spirit and character to it, we have boldly projected the roof, and ornamented the eaves. To give expression to the tame line of roof, we have added a small gable in front. The window pierced in this gable, will serve to light and render useful an additional room in the garret. For the meagre and insufficient porch, we have substituted a veranda ten feet wide, along the whole front; the shade and comfort of which in summer, makes it at least equal in value to any room in the house.

A part of the roof of this veranda, viz: that portion under the shadow of the gable, is finished with a tight sealed floor, so as to form an agreeable balcony to the central window of the front. The windows themselves, (though this is not so important,) we should prefer to change from the common form, to that of the more expressive and cottage-like *latticed sash*, as shown in the engraving.

We think no one can compare these two buildings without confessing that the alteration confers a character of taste and picturesqueness on what was before a very ordinary and insipid building. The improvement does not involve any material change in the body of the house itself, but merely in those external parts easily altered

2   VIEW OF THE SAME, IMPROVED

and added to.

Let us add a few words on the details themselves, that we may be the better understood. The roof should project two and a half feet all round the house. This projection is easily made by taking off the siding directly under the eaves of the old roof—introducing pieces of joists as rafters; upon which, carry out the rafter boarding, and piece out the roof to the necessary breadth.

The verge boards, or eave boards, (i. e. the ornamental piece running round below the outer edge of the roof,) must be cut out of sound *two inch* plank. It is the besetting architectural sin of half the carpenters in the country, (and more especially those in New-England,) to make these portions of a rural cottage of *thin boards.* Nothing gives a cottage, otherwise good, such a rickety, *paste-board-ish* air. The spirit of the carvings and ornaments of the gothic villa, of which these cottages are modified forms, is that of elegant solidity—not "*gingerbread*" flimsiness.

The supports of the veranda are simple solid posts or columns, six or eight inches in diameter, left square for base and capital, and hewn to an octagon in the shaft. The arch which runs at the top, from one to the other, is cut from two inch plank.

Nothing is heavier and less agreeable than the common square chimney. We would therefore advise the owner of *figure* 1 to complete the alteration by adopting the simple form of carrying up distinct flues, standing on a common base, and connected at the top, as we have shown in *figure* 2 The expense is but little more than in the common mode, and the effect far lighter and more agreeable.

ESTIMATE.—The cost of the proposed alteration of this house, will vary from $400 to $700. The cost of lumber and of the mechanic's labor, varies so widely in the different States, that it is impossible to give an estimate which will be an accurate one, for any two sections of the country. Where we write, the whole could be completed in a workmanlike manner, for about $550.

Calvert Vaux, VILLAS AND COTTAGES, 1857

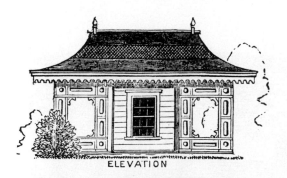

ELEVATION

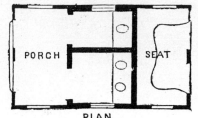

PORCH SEAT

PLAN

Out·Building

Samuel Sloan, HOMESTEAD ARCHITECTURE, 1861

Pump

Byron David Halstead, BARN PLANS & OUTBUILDINGS, 1881

George E. & F.W. Woodward, ARCHITECTURE, LANDSCAPE GARDENING AND RURAL ART, 1867

Fig. 1

A Tool-House, Etc.

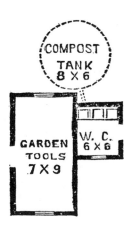

COMPOST TANK 8 × 6

GARDEN TOOLS 7 × 9

W. C. 6 × 6

PLAN.

Garden Implements

The tool-shed is an important and necessary appendage to a well kept garden. The following list includes such implements as are generally needed in private gardens:

THE WHEELBARROW, (Fig. 2).—The wheelbarrow is

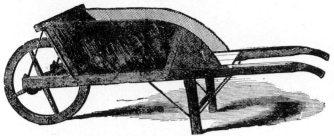

Fig. 2.—GARDEN WHEELBARROW.

an important vehicle in the garden, for the moving of soils, carrying manures, and for conveying the products of the vegetable garden to the house or place of storage, and numerous other purposes. It may be purchased of different sizes and styles, or can be "home-made" by those possessing a little mechanical skill.

THE SPADE, (Fig. 3).—The uses of the spade in a garden are too obvious, and general, to need description. The best in use are Ames' cast-steel, which are light, strong, and durable, and work clean and bright.

THE SHOVEL, (Fig. 4).—The shovel is used for loading, and for mixing and spreading composts and short manures. They are made with long or short handles.

THE DIGGING FORK, (Fig. 5), or Forking Spade, is used instead of a spade to dig in manures, to loosen the earth about the roots of trees, or for taking up root crops; being less liable to cut or injure them than the spade. It is often

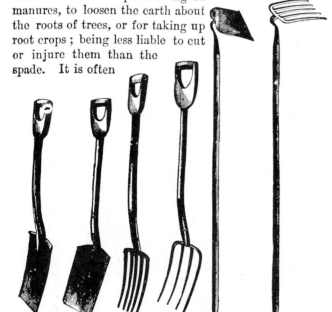

Fig. 3. Fig. 4. Fig. 5. Fig. 6. Fig. 7. Fig. 8.

used instead of the spade, as by its aid the soil can be more readily broken and pulverized.

THE MANURE FORK, (Fig. 6).—Is made of cast-steel with from four to six prongs, and is used for mixing, loading, and spreading manures, work which could not be efficiently done without it.

THE COMMON OR DRAW HOE.—There are several patterns of draw hoes, but the one in general use is the common square hoe, as represented in fig. 7. Its uses in the garden are manifold, and it has frequently to do duty for several other implements. Its principle uses are to clean the surface of the ground from weeds, to open trenches for seeds, and to cover them.

THE PRONG HOE, (Fig. 8).—This is one of the most useful of all garden tools, and is far superior to the blade hoe for stirring and pulverizing the soil. It cannot, it is true, be used where weeds have been allowed to grow to any considerable hight, but then we claim that in all well regulated gardens, weeds should never be allowed to grow so large that they cannot be destroyed by the prong hoe.

THE DUTCH OR PUSH HOE, (Fig. 9), is sometimes preferred to the preceding for cutting the weeds between the rows of vegetables, a work which can be done very quickly by its aid;

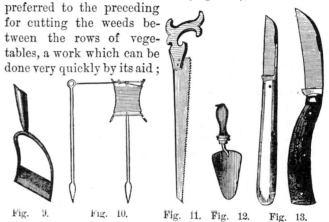

Fig. 9. Fig. 10. Fig. 11. Fig. 12. Fig. 13.

it is not so generally useful as the draw hoe, but is better for the special purposes of destroying weeds.

THE REEL AND LINE, (Fig. 10), are necessary in every well regulated garden, enabling us to plant in straight and accurate rows. The line should be of strong hemp, and is wound upon the reel when not in use.

THE PRUNING SAW, (Fig. 11), is used for cutting off branches that are too large for the knife, for removing dead ones, etc. It can be had in various sizes, from fourteen to twenty inches in length.

THE GARDEN TROWEL, (Fig. 12), is used for setting the smaller kinds of plants when transferred from pots to the open ground; for transplanting annuals and many other uses, it is a very necessary little implement.

PRUNING AND BUDDING KNIVES, (Fig. 13), are necessary to every gardener. They are of different sizes and shapes, for the various purposes of grafting, budding, etc., and are made of the best steel.

GRAPE SCISSORS.—These are slender-pointed scissors, used for thinning out the berries of foreign grapes when

Fig. 14.—LAWN SCYTHE.

they are about half grown, so that those that are left may have room to develop. This operation should never

Peter Henderson, GARDENING FOR PLEASURE, 1875

be neglected if large berries and well shaped bunches are desired.

FLOWER GATHERERS.—A very useful article; the scissors cutting off, and at the same time holding fast the flower or fruit after it is cut, thus enabling one to reach much farther.

LAWN SCYTHES, (Fig. 14).—The lawn scythe is now but little used, the lawn mower taking its place, unless on hill-sides or among trees or shrubs, where the lawn mower cannot be worked.

LAWN MOWERS, (Fig. 15).—The great improvements made in Lawn Mowers during the past few years, and the low price at which they may now be obtained, have made their introduction common to every garden. They are of many sizes, from the small machine that can be easily worked by a boy,

Fig. 15.—LAWN MOWER.

and admirably adapted for city garden plots, to the large horse mowers, that may be daily seen in use in our larger parks. We have in use both the "Excelsior" and "Archimedean" Lawn Mowers, and have found them excellent in all respects.

THE GARDEN ROLLER, (Fig. 16), is indispensable to a well kept lawn, and should always follow after mowing, keeping the ground level and compact; and after gravel walks have been raked over, the roller is necessary to smooth them down.

THE WOODEN LAWN RAKE, (Fig. 17), is used for raking off lawns previous to and after using the scythe or lawn mower, and for removing dead leaves and other rubbish.

Fig. 16.—ROLLER.

THE RAKE, (Fig. 18), is used to level the surface of the ground after it has been spaded or hoed, and to prepare it for the reception of seeds or plants. Rakes are made of different sizes, for convenience in using between rows of plants, with from six to sixteen teeth. When a crop like cabbages is newly planted, we use the rake in preference to anything else, as raking over the surface before the weeds start to grow, destroys the germ of the weed, never allowing it to appear at all.

THE GRASS EDGING KNIFE, (Fig. 19), is used for cutting the grass edgings of flower-beds, its rounded edge fitting into curved lines, for which the spade would be unsuitable.

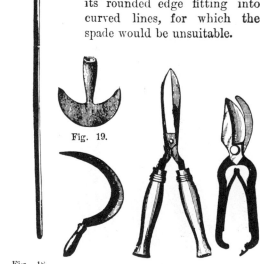

Fig. 19.

Fig. 17.   Fig. 18.   Fig. 20.   Fig. 21.   Fig. 22.

THE SICKLE, (Fig. 20).—This is a most useful implement for switching around and trimming off grass, in places where the scythe or lawn mower cannot be used, or where the place to be cut is small.

HEDGE SHEARS, (Fig. 21), are better fitted for clip-

A.J. Downing, THE HORTICULTURIST, 1846

Dwarf Pear Tree

ping hedges than the Bill Hook, sometimes used for the purpose, particularly in inexperienced hands. A line should be set at the hight to which the hedge is to be cut, as a guide to work by.

HAND-PRUNING SHEARS, (Fig. 22). —These are very efficient and useful; they will cut off a small branch as clean as if a knife had been used. They are indispensable in pruning small fruit-trees and vines, and for use in the grapery and garden.

POLE OR TREE PRUNING SHEARS, (Fig. 23). — These shears are attached to a pole, and operated by means of a lever moved by a cord or a wire; they enable one to cut off branches from trees, shrubbery, etc., that are beyond the reach of the ordinary pruning shears.

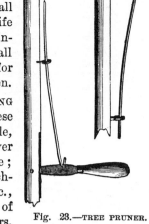

Fig. 23.—TREE PRUNER.

Branches of an inch and a half in diameter may be easily cut off with this instrument.

GARDEN SYRINGE, (Fig. 24).—The syringe is in

Fig. 24.—GARDEN SYRINGE.

daily use in the greenhouse or conservatory, where syringing is necessary to keep the plants in a flourishing and healthy condition. They are made of several sizes and patterns, and fitted with roses for dispersing water with varying force.

WATERING-POT.—A watering-pot is indispensable in the greenhouse or conservatory, where it is daily needed. It should be obtained of a suitable size, from one to four gallons, with a rose for sprinkling, which may be detached at will.

THE EXCELSIOR PUMP, (Fig. 25), is a very compact and useful implement for greenhouse and garden work. It is easily operated, and throws a continuous stream. It is very effective for watering shrubbery, gardens, or lawns, and may be used in an emergency as a fire extinguisher and prevent a conflagration.

Fig. 25.—EXCELSIOR PUMP.

THE SIDNEY SEED-SOWER, (Fig. 26).—This is a very useful implement, enabling

Fig. 26.

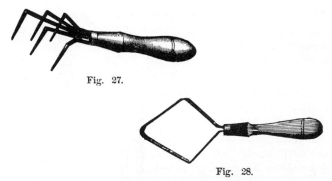

Fig. 27.

Fig. 31.

Fig. 28.

the operator to sow seeds with perfect regularity, especially in wet or windy weather. It will distribute large or small seeds with equal regularity, either broadcast or in drills or pots.

THE EXCELSIOR WEEDING HOOK, (Fig. 27), is a very handy implement for removing weeds from among small and tender plants, and for stirring up the soil. It can be used between rows of seedlings, ornamental plants, or

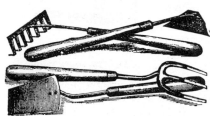

Fig. 29.—SMALL GARDEN SET.

wherever it is desirable to remove weeds, without injury to the plants or soiling the hands.

NOYES' HAND WEEDER, (Fig. 28), is a kind of miniature hand hoe, and is very convenient and useful for working between plants, dressing pots, and cleaning away weeds, where a large hoe could not be used to good advantage.

LADIES' AND CHILDRENS' GARDEN TOOLS, (Fig. 29).—In all flower gardens there is a great deal of hand-work to be done. This lot of small implements consisting of a spade, fork, rake, and hoe, will be found very useful in working on small flower borders.

Fig. 30.—STEP LADDER.

STEP LADDERS, (Fig. 30).—The step-ladder is always useful in a garden, especially during the fruiting season. It is made in different sizes, varying from three to ten feet, and weighing from ten to thirty pounds; it is made with flat steps, so that a person may stand upon them while working, and can be extended or contracted as required. For use amongst large trees, in the orchard, a much greater length of ladder is required, and there are various forms of orchard ladders in use, but the step-ladder is sufficient for all ordinary garden uses.

HAND-GLASSES.—The uses of these have been mentioned under cauliflowers, cucumber, etc. Home-made hand-glasses, being simply a

small frame covered with a pane of glass, are very useful, but as they exclude some light they are not equal to those made with glass all around. Hand-glasses with metal frames and glass sides and top, are made of different sizes and styles, one of the more elaborate of which is shown in fig. 31. Though somewhat expensive, they will, if carefully used, last many years.

Trellises, or supports for plants, are needed in the flower and vegetable garden not only for climbers, but for keeping plants which have weak stems within proper bounds. Trellises for pots may be purchased ready-made, as may those for climbing roses and such plants; they are usually made of rattan upon a frame of light wooden stakes, and some are made entirely of wire. A person of a mechanical turn can readily make all that will be needed.

Fig. 32.

A few engravings are given here as suggestions. Fig. 32 shows a useful support made with a barrel hoop and staves; the same plan may be carried out with two or more hoops, and laths, if staves are too heavy. This will answer for tomatoes, raspberries, and various other plants. A more permanent tomato trellis is shown in fig. 33, in which slats are supported by Λ shaped uprights. If put together with screws, such a trellis may be carefully put away in the fall

Fig. 33.—TOMATO TRELLIS.

and made to last several years. A rustic trellis, like that in fig. 34, is often useful in the flower garden, or it may serve when covered with climbers to divide the flower from the vegetable garden. It is made of sticks of cedar or other durable wood, set as shown in the engraving, and tied where the bars cross one another with strong tarred twine. With these examples

Fig. 34.—RUSTIC TRELLIS.

as suggestions, one will find no difficulty in making more elaborate supports and with other materials.

Country House For Any Climate

A LITTLE examination into the merits of this design, as illustrated by the engravings of elevation and ground-plans, will satisfy any one that our title, if not entirely elegant, has not been chosen without some attention to the correctness of its application. While we are well aware that it is next to impossible to prepare plans embracing all the conditions made imperative by a great diversity of climate, we are not less sensible that compromises can be effected, greatly extending the application of a given plan with but a limited amount of local modifications. To the Southern projector who may conceive a partiality for the idea here illustrated, we would say, give outside blinds and umbrage to all the windows, and build a detached kitchen, and you have a complete Southern house for a family of moderate size. The through hall, which effectually cuts off the dining apartment from the parlor and library, is a very liberal arrangement for a house of this size; and indeed this circumstance, combined with its peculiar application in the plan before us, is the basis of the compromise here intended between the varieties of climate.

ACCOMMODATION.—The hall A, fig. 2, entered from a neat front veranda, is 9 feet wide, and contains the principal staircase. The parlor B is 16 by 22 feet. By opening the sliding doors, the eye is greeted by the pleasing view of an octagonal bay-window; this is an appendage to the apartment C, a room 16 feet square, which would make a delightful sitting-room or library, according to the choice of the occupants. The dining-room D has two snug little china closets. The kitchen E, 14 by 10 feet, has a closet and flight of private stairs. On the second floor, fig. 3, we find three good chambers, F, provided with closets, and two smaller ones, H and G, the latter entered from the private stairs.

CONSTRUCTION.—Brick, stone, or wood are equally applicable to construction of this dwelling. If ordinary bricks or rubble-stone are used, it should be stuccoed; if built of wood, the framing should be boarded in the horizontal manner, the angles or corner posts being cased with vertical strips 5 or 6 inches wide, against which the abutting joint of the weatherboarding is made. A roof of shingles or slate is equally admissible, due provision having been made in the framing of the rafters for the greater weight of the latter. The execution of the joinery with well selected and seasoned wood, say white pine or cypress doors and dressings, yellow pine stairs with walnut hand-rail, etc., would be a satisfactory mode of internal finish.

ESTIMATE.—We put the cost of this, under the most favorable circumstances, at $4300.

Samuel Sloan, HOMESTEAD ARCHITECTURE, 1861

1

2
PRINCIPAL FLOOR.

3
SECOND FLOOR.

Outside Color

We are not among those who cast off, and on a sudden condemn, as out of all good taste, the time-honored white house with its green blinds, often so tastefully gleaming out from beneath the shade of summer trees; nor do we doggedly adhere to it, except when in keeping, by contrast or otherwise, with everything around it. For a century past white has been the chief color of our wooden houses, and often so of brick ones, in the United States. This color has been supposed to be strong and durable, being composed chiefly of white lead; and as it *reflected* the rays of the sun instead of *absorbing* them, as some of the darker colors do, it was thus considered a better preserver of the weather-boarding from the cracks which the fervid heat of the sun is apt to make upon it, than the darker colors. White, consequently, has always been considered, until within a few years past, as a fitting and *tasteful* color for dwellings, both in town and country. A new school of *taste* in colors has risen, however, within a few years past, among us; about the same time, too, that the recent gingerbread and beadwork style of country building was introduced. And these were both, as all *new* things are apt to be, carried to extremes. Instead of *toning* down the glare of the white into some quiet, neutral shade, as a straw color; a drab of different hues — always an agreeable and appropriate color for a dwelling, particularly when the door and window casings are dressed with a deeper or lighter shade, as those shades predominate in the main body of the house; or a natural and soft *wood* color, which also may be of various shades; or even the warm russet hue of some of our rich stones — quite appropriate, too, as applied to wood, or bricks — the *fashion* must be followed without either rhyme or reason, and hundreds of our otherwise pretty and imposing country houses have been daubed over with the dirtiest, gloomiest pigment imaginable, making every habitation which it touched look more like a funeral appendage than a cheerful, life-enjoying home We candidly say that we have no sort of affection for such sooty daubs. The fashion which dictates them is a barbarous, false, and arbitrary fashion; void of all natural taste in its inception; and to one who has a cheerful, life-loving spirit about him, such colors have no more fitness on his dwelling or out-buildings, than a tomb would have in his lawn or dooryard.

Locality, amplitude of the buildings, the purpose to which they are applied — every consideration connected with them, in fact, should be consulted, as to color. Stone will give its own color; which, by the way, some prodigiously smart folks *paint* — quite as decorous or essential, as to " paint the lily." Brick sometimes must be painted, but it should be of a color in keeping with its character, — of substance and dignity; not a counterfeit of stone, or to cheat him who looks upon it into a belief that it may be marble, or other unfounded pretension. A *warm* russet is most appropriate for brick-work of any kind of color — the color of a russet apple, or undressed leather

Red and yellow are both too glaring, and slate, or lead colors too somber and cold. It is, in fact, a strong argument in favor of bricks in building, where they can be had as cheap as stone or wood, that any color can be given to them which the good taste of the builder may require, in addition to their durability, which, when made of good material, and properly burned, is quite equal to stone. In a wooden structure one may play with his fancy in the way of color, minding in the operation, that he does not play the mountebank, and like the clown in the circus, make his tattooed tenement the derision of men of correct taste, as the other does his burlesque visage the ridicule of his auditors.

A *wooden* country house, together with its out-buildings, should always be of a cheerful and softly-toned color — a color giving a feeling of warmth and comfort; nothing glaring or flashy about it. And yet, such buildings should not, in their color, any more than in their architecture, appear as if *imitating* either stone or brick. Wood, of itself, is light. One cannot build a *heavy* house of wood, as compared with brick or stone. Therefore all imitation or device which may lead to a belief that it may be other than what it really is, is nothing less than a fraud — not criminal, we admit, but none the less a fraud upon good taste and architectural truth.

It is true that in this country we cannot afford to place in stone and brick buildings those ornate trimmings and appendages which, perhaps, if economy were not to be consulted, might be more durably constructed of stone, but at an expense too great to be borne by those of moderate means. Yet it is not essential that such appendages should be of so expensive material. The very purposes to which they are applied, as a parapet, a railing, a balustrade, a portico, piazza, or porch; all these may be of wood, even when the material of the house *proper* is of the most durable kind; and by being painted in keeping with the building itself, produce a fine effect, and do no violence to good taste or the most fastidious propriety. They may be even sanded to a color, and grained, stained, or otherwise brought to an identity, almost, with the material of the house, and be quite proper, because they simply are *appendages* of convenience, necessity, or luxury, to the building itself, and may be taken away without injuring or without defacing the main structure. They are not a *material* part of the building itself, but reared for purposes which may be dispensed with. It is a matter of taste or preference, that they were either built there, or that they remain permanently afterward, and of consequence, proper that they be of wood. Yet they should not *imitate* stone or brick. They should still show that they *are* of wood, but in color and outside preservation denote that they are appendages to a *stone* or *brick* house, by complying with the proper shades in color which predominate in the building itself, and become their own subordinate character.

Not being a professional painter, or compounder of colors, we shall offer no receipts or specifics for painting or washing buildings. Climate affects the composition of both paints and washes, and those who are competent in this line, are the proper persons to dictate their various compositions; and we do but common justice to the skill and intelligence of our numerous mechanics, when we recommend to those who contemplate building, to apply forthwith to such as are masters of their trade for all the information they require on the various subjects connected with it. One who sets out to be his own architect, builder, and painter, is akin to the lawyer in the proverb, who has a fool for his client, when pleading his own case, and quite as apt to have quack in them all. Hints, general outlines, and oftentimes matters of detail in interior convenience, and many other minor affairs may be given by the proprietor, when he is neither a professional architect, mechanic, or even an amateur; but in all things affecting the *substantial* and important parts of his buildings, he should consult those who are proficient and experienced in the department on which he consults them. And it may perhaps be added that none *professing* to be such, are competent, unless well instructed, and whose labors have met the approbation of those competent to judge.

There is one kind of color, prevailing to a great extent in many parts of our country, particularly the northern and eastern, which, in its effect upon any one having an eye to a fitness of things in country buildings, is a monstrous perversion of good taste. That is the glaring red, made up of Venetian red, ochre, or Spanish brown, with doors and windows touched off with white. The only apology we have ever heard given for such a barbarism was, that it is a good, strong, and lasting color. We shall not go into an examination as to that fact, but simply answer, that if it be so, there are other colors, not more expensive, which are equally strong and durable, and infinitely more tasteful and fitting. There can be nothing less comporting with the simplicity of rural scenery, than a glaring red color on a building. It *connects* with nothing natural about it; it neither *fades* into any surrounding shade of soil or vegetation, and must of necessity, stand out in its own bold and unshrouded impudence, a perfect Ishmaelite in color, and a perversion of every thing harmonious in the design. We eschew *red*, therefore, from every thing in rural architecture.

Lewis F. Allen, RURAL ARCHITECTURE, 1862

Study For Cottage Roof Alteration

Calvert Vaux, VILLAS AND COTTAGES, 1857

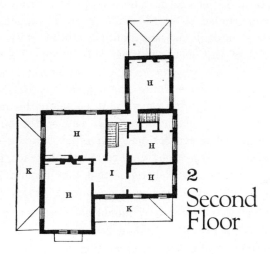

Samuel Sloan, HOMESTEAD ARCHITECTURE, 1861

An Irregular Bracketed Country House

We might, with almost equal propriety, have termed this a farm-house. The only objection to this is the probability of impressing the reader with the idea that its application would be accordingly restricted. Indeed, it almost deserves the name of VILLA; but the total absence of ostentation in its external aspect inclines us to the appellation we have bestowed upon it, notwithstanding the villa-like extent of its accommodations. Plain, sensible, and solid, it is within the reach and applicable to the circumstances of many who love convenience without ambitious display, and who prefer dignified plainness to gingerbread ostentation. Architecturally, this design aims at being a country dwelling, manifesting the dignity, comfort, and substantial character of social life that is attainable in the country. There is a growing demand for this class of dwellings. Farmers are becoming rich, merchants and manufacturers are retiring from business; and we know that while the frank modesty of the farmer seldom allows him to aspire to towers or pinnacles, nine out of ten of retired citizens are too plain and practical in their views to seek for more than the embodiment of the various accommodations suited to their modes of life, at the lowest grade of expense requisite to give them a tasteful and substantial home. Since we have held these points in view, our motive for the comprehensive appellation "country-house" will be at once perceived. Suggestive not only of home comfort, but of the pleasure of social existence, the internal arrangements are in conformity to the demands of a life of business or a life of leisure, while the outward evidence, furnished by the elevation, goes far to sustain the idea that the proprietor, if not in possession of an unlimited store of wealth, has been touched by the spirit of elevated taste, and has declared his inspiration in language susceptible of no double meaning.

ACCOMMODATION.—A veranda G, fig. 1, furnishes the entrance way to the main hall D. A drawing-room A, 14 by 26 feet, entered by folding doors from the hall, forms a very interesting portion of this plan, on account of relative situation, its modest little bay-window, and the adjoining veranda, which is approached through lengthened windows, and communicates in the same manner with the sitting-room. This sitting-room, marked B, is 22 by 14 feet, and

communicates directly with the drawing-room **and** main hall. This hall is 12 feet square, and a passage, containing the main stairway, leads to the **rear** entrance, and affords communication with the kitchen and private stairs. An arch thrown over the **stair** passage, at its junction with the hall D, will give the latter a complete individuality, and will be not only productive of effect as a feature, but gives opportunity for the introduction of a separate and dissimilar cornice, and, in short, establishes for the main hall a character exclusively its own.

A dining-room, 17 by 24 feet, furnished with china closet, and entered from the main hall, is located in the front portion of the house. With the facilities attendant on the mode of service which generally obtains in the style of living of which this house is assumed to be an exponent, all the fixtures of the table can be promptly removed, and the apartment, under the auspices of youthful management, becomes a scene of social and even sportive enjoyment. The private stairs are situated between the dining-room and kitchen, communicating with a small lobby, which is intended for a passage between these apartments. The kitchen E, 14 by 20 feet, is provided with a side entrance, and a very respectable appendage, 12 by 14 feet, which may be used as a pump-shed, wood-house, or bakery. In the latter case a suitable oven will be built, so as to vent its smoke into the kitchen chimney.

By reference to the plan of the second floor, fig. 2, it will be observed that the chambers are respectively designated by the letter H. I is the hall, and K the roofs of verandas. Good bed-rooms may be fitted up in the *garret*, care being taken to provide for their ventilation, in addition to that afforded by the gable windows.

CONSTRUCTION.—Brick, rough cast, with wooden cornices, and slate or shingle roof, may be indicated as the essential components of this structure. The verandas, however, require metallic roofing. The window-heads and sills should be stone. There is no absolute objection to building the walls of rubble-stone. The effect of this would be to make it look more essentially the home of the farmer "to the manor born."

ESTIMATE.—Built in the manner above described, the cost of this dwelling would not vary much from $7500.

DESIGN FOR STABLE, ETC.

Vignettes

Calvert Vaux, VILLAS AND COTTAGES, 1857

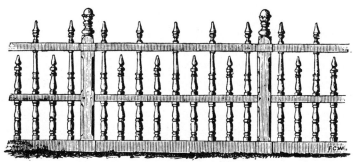

ELEVATION OF FENCE.

VERGE-BOARD.

DESIGN FOR PARTIALLY INCLOSED VERANDA.

Ornamental Planting

A.J. Downing, LANDSCAPE GARDENING, 1841

J.J. Thomas, REGISTER OF RURAL AFFAIRS, 1860

OUNTRY homes are of two kinds—the repulsive and the beautiful. The former are occupied by those who know nothing of domestic enjoyment, and who seek happiness in the bar-room and grog-shop. They never see any charms in the works of nature—ornamental shrubbery to them is "brush," and flowers are only "weeds." They never plant a rose-bush nor a shade tree. They sometimes set out a few apple and cherry trees. But these are left to take care of themselves, and what remain after ten years, appear like those shown in figure 1, instead of attaining the perfection seen in figure 2, as

Fig. 1.

Fig. 2.

they would have done if well managed and properly cultivated. They have an especial contempt for all ornamental trees, and exclaim,

FERGUSON. ALBANY

Fig. 3—*Premises of the Man "who Cares nothing for Looks" nor for the Comforts of Home.*

"What! set out trees that don't bear anything fit to eat—that are only good to look at!" Their dwellings are bleak and desolate. There is nothing about them attractive to their children, who grow up with no attachment to home, and with little appreciation of the social virtues. The first figure on this page, (fig. 3,) is a representation of all that is inviting in the homes of their childhood, and where from the earliest

FERGUSON ALBANY

Fig. 4—*Premises of the Man who makes Home attractive to his Children.*

dawn of their forming minds, they have received most of their impressions of life. Few of them have been able to surmount these discouraging influences, and they have become coarse and unintelligent. How different might have been their character if they had been brought up under the influences of the other home represented on the same page!

This neat cottage (fig. 4) cost no more in the first place than the dilapidated one. Its owner kept it in perfect repair, and planted and cultivated the encircling grounds during those spare moments that his neighbor who lives in the other, occupied at the tavern. Each house cost nearly a thousand dollars in building; while the planting and cultivation of the grounds about the latter, did not require an expenditure of fifty dollars.

There is now scarcely an intelligent mind who does not admit for the above reasons, the real and substantial value and utility of ornamental planting. Added to its utility, is the fascinating employment of imitating the most beautiful natural groupings of objects, by planting and arranging trees. With all these inducements, great and increased attention should be given to the subject, and it would open a world of exalted enjoyment to those who pursue it. Most fortunately, it does not require necessarily a profuse expenditure of money. As much skill may be employed in decorating the limited grounds of a cottage, at an expense within fifty dollars, as in laying out and planting a magnificent park of hundreds of acres, costing many ten thousands.

Much money is wasted in attempts to ornament the grounds of a dwelling before a well digested plan has been adopted. Alterations alone have sometimes cost more than the execution of a complete well arranged design. We have known owners to expend more in excavating and in building terraces, with a real injury in appearance, than others would in effecting the most finished improvement. In one instance the owner of a suburban residence, with the constant labor of two gardeners, succeeded in accomplishing less in the way of neat and beautiful appearance, than another with the services of a single gardener but two days in each week. The art of ornamental planting cannot be learned in a single day, but like any other art, requires much thought and study, with all the assistance that may be derived from the experience of others. Those who wish to understand the subject completely are referred to Downing, Sargent, and Kemp, for full instructions; but a short article like this may perhaps afford many useful hints to those who cannot give so much time to the subject, or whose moderate grounds and limited means may not warrant great expenditure.

In offering suggestions on this subject, it will be best to begin at the beginning, and lay down briefly a few rules for selecting a site for a dwelling. The following requisites may be regarded as important nearly in the order in which they are named, but some will transpose them more or less, according to their preferences.

1. Healthfulness.
2. Neighborhood.
3. Soil and climate.
4. Suitable site, convenience of access, &c.
5. Scenery and views.

The first is all-important, as no home comforts can atone for ruined health. The second is scarcely inferior, for a family possessing civilization and refinement cannot properly enjoy themselves when constantly exposed to the petty annoyances of vulgar and pilfering neighbors, and who are shut out entirely from the social enjoyment of such as are of a congenial character. Where a whole neighborhood unites in works for public benefit and moral improvement, the very atmosphere seems purer and more delightful, than where semi-barbarism and selfishness are the ruling influences. A *fertile soil* is all-essential to the resident who would obtain the necessaries and comforts of life from his own land; and a climate favorable to the cultivation of the finer fruits is equally so to every one who expects to enjoy a constant circle of these most wholesome and delicious luxuries. The *site*, and suitable conveniences for access, are important considerations. A low, foggy place, will be unhealthful; a high one, without shelter, will be bleak and cold; if very near a public road, it will be exposed to noise, dust, and obtrusive observation; if remote from the road, much needless traveling will be required, and not a little inconvenience will be found in time of deep snows. A gentle eminence, and a moderate distance from the public road, and the shelter of evergreens on the side of prevailing winds, will obviate most of these difficulties. A quiet side-road branching from a main highway, will often be better than directly on a great thoroughfare. Comparative nearness to places of public worship, to schools, a post-office, mill and railroad station, are each of considerable importance, and should all be taken into consideration. The value of *fine scenery* will be variously estimated; some would prize it as all-essential, while others would scarcely think of it. Some would merely covet a showy situation as seen from the nearest highway, in order to draw the admiration of travelers; others, discarding such motives, would only desire beautiful views from the windows of the dwelling or from the surrounding grounds, in order to make their homes interesting and attractive to their children.

The site having been selected, the next step is to build the house. This portion of labor does not belong to our present subject, but the plan and intentions should be well understood before the exact spot for the house is fixed upon, and its frontings determined. This precaution is essential in order to secure the finest views, and to furnish protection from winds, or from undesirable odors or unsightly objects.

Great progress has been made within a few years in the art of ornamental planting, but it is still so common to witness defects, that to point out some of these defects in the first place, will more fitly prepare the way for specific directions.

The most common error of past years, but now rapidly disappearing, is the practice of planting only in straight lines or geometric figures. Absolute stiffness reigned supreme, in the attempt to avoid any approach towards *irregularity*. A neighbor, intelligent in other things, when he saw the first specimen of the natural mode of planting, exclaimed, " Why, Mr. T.! you have none of your trees in rows!" He considered a want of straight lines a striking evidence of a bungler. The geometric style not only required this formal regularity, but *symmetry*, as it was termed, demanded that every object should have its corresponding one. A tree on one side must oppose just such a tree on the other side; a row on the right was to have its accompanying row on the left. It is stated that the old gardener of the Earl of Selkirk, was so strongly imbued with this mania for symmetry, that when he shut up the thief who stole his fruit in one summer-house, he was compelled for the sake of symmetry, to put his own son in the other opposite. How immeasurably more pleasing and beautiful than this stiff and artificial mode, is the simple imitation of the beautiful and picturesque in nature, which constitutes the modern or natural style of planting.

It is not an unfrequent error to suppose that the modern style consists *merely* in *irregularity*. But irregularity without arrangement, is not taste—confusion is not the beautiful in nature. The *perfection* of art consists in producing a pleasing effect, while the art which produced it is concealed from the eye of the spectator. The scenery which artificial planting produces, may *appear* to be the accidental arrangement of agreeable parts or objects; but it must really be the result of close study and a careful eye—in the same way that the roughly dashed work of a skillful painter, where every touch, rude and accidental as it may seem at first glance, is found on taking the whole together, to produce a most perfect and complete combination of different parts. And one great excellence of the modern style consists in its complete adaptation to all grades of residences—it does not require costly embellishments, nor a profuse outlay—the cottage resident may show as much skill in a *tasteful simplicity*, as the owner of the magnificent park in the disposition of his broad lawns and majestic forest trees.

In order to produce the best effect in grouping trees, these requisites are essential—*unity, harmony*, and *variety*. The following is an example

Fig. 5—*Example in Grouping.*

in illustration (fig. 5)—and the scene represented in fig. 6 on the following page, exhibiting a natural group of elms, possesses everything agreeable

Fig. 6—*Grouping Elms.*

but *variety*—and it possesses much of this quality so far as the arrangement of the trees is concerned, but it lacks variety from the trees being all of one kind.   For this reason the preceding example (fig. 5) is free from objection.

The next figure (fig. 7) affords an illustration of monotonous irregularity; and presents the same appearance that some grounds do after they have grown up with trees which have been planted all over without regard to effect or to open portions of lawn, or distant views

Fig. 7—*Monotonous Grouping.*

towards beautiful objects.   On the other hand, the two following figures present fine examples of natural grouping; the first (fig. 8) exhibiting the advantage which may be taken of slight undulations in the ground, in increasing the picturesque variety which it may afford; and the second (fig. 9) a fine and exceedingly varied sky outline produced by a group of dissimilar trees, yet all supporting each other and harmonizing together.

No error is more common with those who have "a *little* knowledge" on the subject of planting and designing grounds, than in attempting to combine within the limits of a small place, all the different objects that

Fig. 8.

can be introduced only in extensive grounds. Neat and harmonious
simplicity is sacrificed to incongruous confusion. This propensity is

Fig. 9.

sarcastically exhibited by Lowell in his account of the "*Rural Cot of
Mr. Knott,*" a dwelling

> "'Twixt twelve feet square of garden plot,
>   And twelve feet more of lawn,"

containing meadow and upland, a water view, (consisting of pump and
trough,) and a woodland made up of

> "Three pines stuck up askew,
>   Two dead ones and a live one."

The house was built cheaply of wood, and painted in imitation of stone;
but so much was expended on odd conceits and flimsy ornaments, that

> "Ere many days poor Knott began
>   Perforce accepting draughts that ran
>   All ways—except up chimney;

> The house, though painted stone to mock,
> With nice white lines round every block,
>   Some trepidation stood in,
> When tempests (with petrific shock,
> So to speak,) made it really rock,
>   Though not a whit less wooden."

Among other errors often committed in the attempt to crowd many objects within a small space, is the construction of a multiplicity of walks, beyond what is useful or essential; planting trees over the whole surface, rendering the grounds uniformly spotted with them; introducing too many flower beds; making artificial mounds or terraces, instead of merely softening off the naturally varying surface; placing rustic objects in immediate connection with the house, the architecture of which does not at all harmonize with them; and especially to be avoided is the error of introducing *shams,* which will be discarded by every person of correct taste. Among these, as Kemp observes, are " artificial ruins, mere fronts to buildings, bridges that have no meaning, and for which there is no necessity," to which we may add all puny attempts at artificial rock work, which are only small heaps of stones.

Persons of more moderate pretensions, including a large portion of such as live on medium-sized farms, fall into another error. They devote to ornamental planting a square plot of ground exactly in front of the dwelling, and varying from half an acre down to two rods square. This is

FERGUSON, ALBANY

Fig. 10—*Residence with a Neat Front Yard only.*

enclosed with a picket fence in the form of a *tight pen,* with one straight walk passing through the center from the front door down to a small gate opening into the public highway. Very few ever pass through this gate or enter through the front door; but carriages, wagons, and foot passengers go in at the large gate just without this square yard, and enter the house by a side or back door. The square yard is therefore often allowed to grow up with grass or weeds, and is shaded by a few cherry trees, one or two lilac bushes, and a few hollyhocks. Occasionally it is seen in much better order, with a straight and neatly-kept gravel walk lined with shrubs and flowers, and with rows of cherry and pear trees on either side—(fig. 10.) This is, however, the only neat portion of the whole premises; for the worm-fence enclosures on the right and left, and the back yard, contain a numerous collection of cord-wood, old rails, empty boxes, barrels and barrel hoops, unburned brush, plows and sleds, wagons and carts, pails and kettles, chips, slop puddles, &c. It appears, however, like a neat and comfortable residence to the traveler who is careful to look at it only at the moment when he is exactly in front.

Plans of Grounds

A small town or village residence, with only a few feet of ground, may be laid out as represented in the accompanying figures. Fig. 11 exhibits

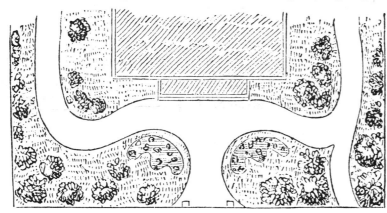

Fig. 11.

a front yard about twice the breadth of the house, and with about fifteen or twenty feet from the front door to the street. Instead of the straight narrow walk too often seen, this is broad, with curved sides, passing on the left to the garden, and on the right to the kitchen and barn. A small gate on the right admits entrance to the kitchen without passing up the front walk, and the curved passage from this side-gate being closely planted with evergreens, is rendered less conspicuous. Fig. 12 is a larger place, admitting greater variety in the form of the walks, and several arabesque flower beds cut in the smooth shaven lawn. The exterior is planted with the larger shrubbery or trees, evergreens standing nearest the boundary, and growing thickly where it is desired to conceal any unsightly neighboring building or other undesirable

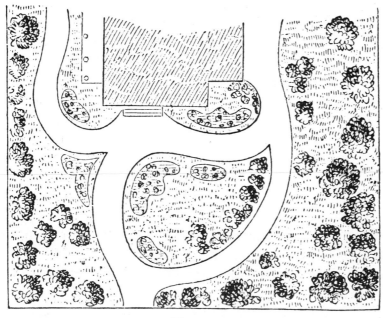

Fig. 12.

object, and leaving an opening where the view is of a pleasing character. In grounds of the limited extent of these two residences, perfect neatness should prevail; the soil should have been previously made deep and rich, that the trees and shrubs may grow freely with rich foliage; the part covered with grass should be smooth, (the grass seed having been sown very thickly, or at the rate of two or three bushels per acre,) and the grass mowed twice a week within half an inch of the surface, during the early part of the season, and once a week later; the gravel walk should be as smooth as a floor, slightly convex or curved upwards, and trimmed with a true curve at the edges.

Fig. 13 exhibits a plan for the grounds of a village residence, varying from half an acre to an acre, and where a horse and cow are kept. The front portion, as far back as the dwelling, is occupied with lawn, kept closely shaven, with trees and shrubs, and a few flower-beds bordering the walks. In the rear and on the left is a small orchard, through which the carraige road passes; and in the yard which it enters is the horse and carriage barn, the cow-house, and poultry-house. On the right is the fruit and kitchen garden. This is laid out so as to admit of plowing at least once a year, as well as horse-cultivation so far as may be desired. The rows of fruit trees are dwarfs, with currants and gooseberries and the other smaller fruits. The boundary of the kitchen garden is planted with roses and flowering shrubs, through which a neatly kept walk passes, thus giving the advantages of a wider extent of ornamental grounds. Converting the kitchen garden into a lawn, and providing a kitchen garden by extending the grounds to the left, would form a more perfect place.

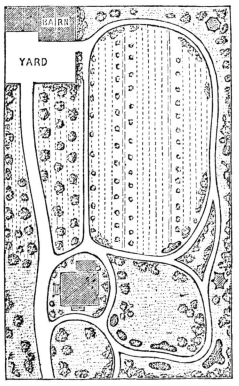

13—*Grounds of a Village Residence.*

A design for the grounds of a farm residence, where half an acre to an acre is devoted to ornamental planting, is exhibited in fig. 14. The carriage road enters nearly in front of the house, bending slightly, and forming a sweep for turning—from this the carriage may return to the road, or pass to the carriage-house in front of the barn-yard. On the left is a pear and cherry orchard planted in the quincunx manner; in front and to the right is the lawn, kept smoothly shaven and planted with trees and shrubs. These grounds are traversed by a curved walk five

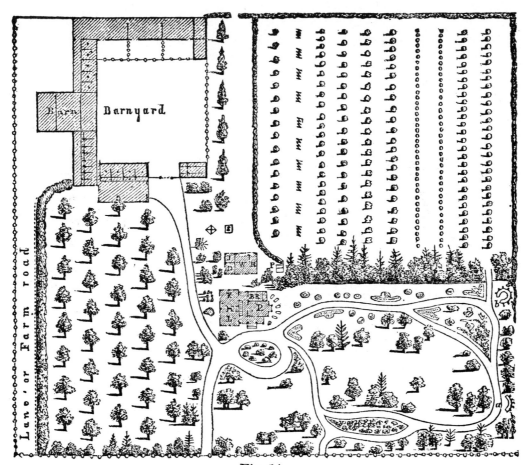

Fig. 14.

and a-half feet wide, which is bordered with several flower-beds. The boundaries are most thickly planted where the view is undesirable beyond; and the view across the lawn is left nearly unobstructed towards the most distant points, and especially towards the seat *a*, and the summer-house *b*. In the rear of the grounds is the garden, which combines the kitchen and fruit garden for dwarf trees. They are planted in rows, and consist of dwarf pears, dwarf apples on doucain stock, gooseberries, currants and raspberries, and dwarf plums. Between these rows the ground is cultivated by horses, the garden vegetables being planted in drills to admit the passage of a narrow cultivator.

DESIGN FOR A FOUNTAIN.

DESIGN FOR A WELL-HOUSE.

George E. & F.W. Woodward, ARCHITECTURE, LANDSCAPE GARDENING AND RURAL ART, 1867

George E. & F.W. Woodward, ARCHITECTURE, LANDSCAPE GARDENING AND RURAL ART, 1867

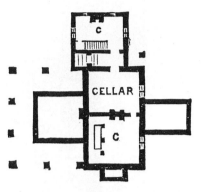

FIG. 1.—CELLAR PLAN.

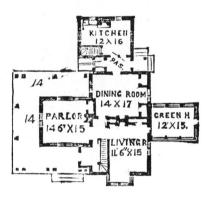

FIG. 2.—FIRST FLOOR.

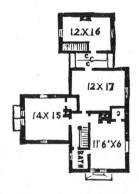

FIG. 3.—SECOND FLOOR.

Cottage

WE show here a compact, convenient cottage, having a conservatory attached for those who love to gratify their taste for flowers. Each room has a cross draft, and can be abundantly ventilated in warm weather. A passage between the kitchen and dining-room cuts off the smell of cooking, and the doors from the kitchen are double, with spring-hinges, and without locks or other fastenings; they are opened with the foot, and close immediately after passing. The servant can pass in the kitchen through one door and out through the other with a large tray of dishes, and thus avoid meeting any one, while flies and the aroma of cooking have little chance of getting into the main part of the house. We think during the summer months it adds much to the comfort of all country houses to put in the windows the neat, modern wire-gauze window-guard, which does not obstruct air or sight, and does keep out effectually flies, millers, gnats, beetles, spiders, mosquitoes, bats, cats, and the whole list of nuisances against which we make our rooms close and dismal, and mope in summer evening darkness to avoid. The safety, cleanliness, and comfort of an open country house, night and day, can thus be enjoyed; light, sunshine, and fresh air can be had in abundance, and a feeling of comfort insured which those who have once tried it would never be without.

FIG. 1.—CELLAR PLAN.

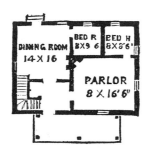

FIG. 2.—FIRST FLOOR.

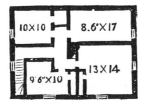

FIG. 3.—SECOND FLOOR.

Cottage

THIS design can, for the amount of room afforded, be constructed very cheaply. The kitchen is shown in the basement plan, but can be put on the first floor, or in a rear addition, if deemed more convenient. If built in an exposed situation, some filling-in between the studding will be necessary. There are several modes of doing this, all of which add to the stiffness and solidity of the frame, and ward off the searching winds. An air chamber for confined or dead air adds much to winter warmth and summer coolness, and this is usually provided for. The most common mode of filling-in is with soft brick laid on edge in mortar; grout is also made use of. Back plastering, or lathing between studs—nailing common laths or rough pieces against strips fastened to each side of the studs and covered with coarse mortar—is serviceable. Where lumber is plenty, cover the frame with rough boards, and put the weather-boarding on the outside of the rough boarding; this we have found answers an excellent purpose. A layer of common tarred roofing-paper between the two courses of boarding will render the house impenetrable to wind or rain, and affords one of the best means of protection.

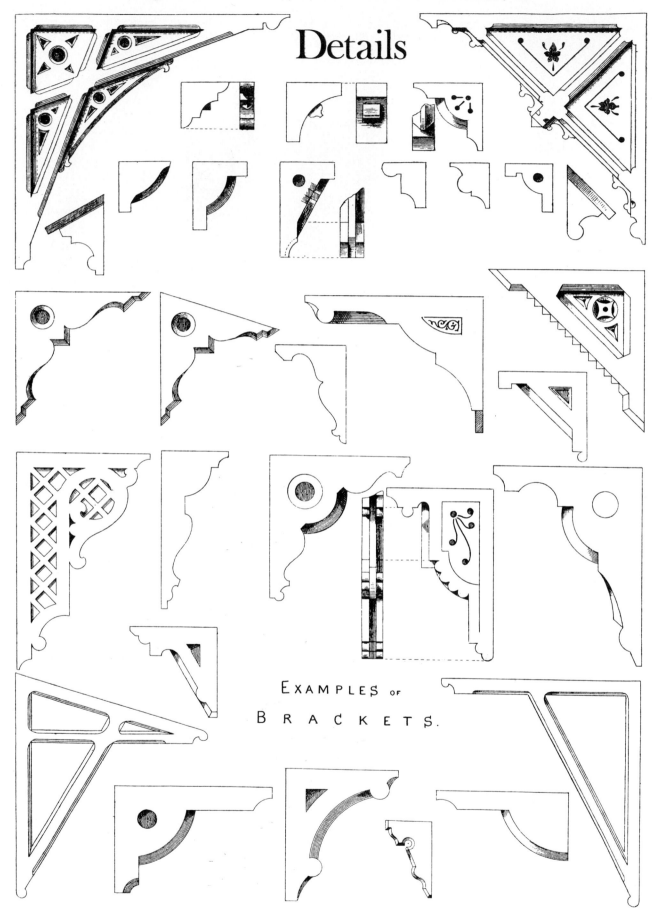

Details

EXAMPLES OF BRACKETS.

Building Details

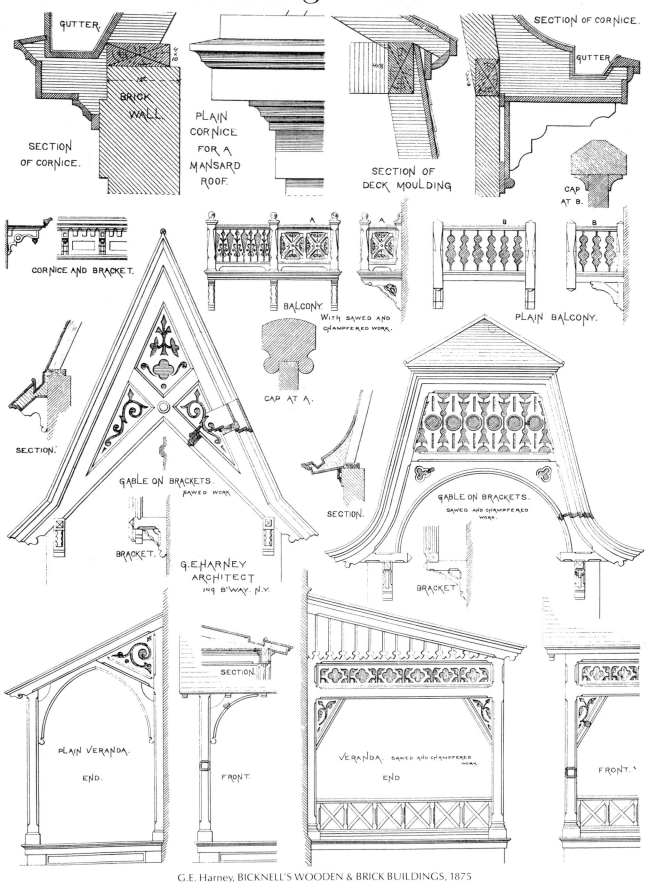

GUTTER.

SECTION OF CORNICE.

BRICK WALL

SECTION OF CORNICE.

PLAIN CORNICE FOR A MANSARD ROOF.

SECTION OF DECK MOULDING

SECTION OF CORNICE.

GUTTER

CAP AT B.

CORNICE AND BRACKET.

BALCONY. WITH SAWED AND CHAMPFERED WORK.

A

A

B

B

PLAIN BALCONY.

SECTION.

GABLE ON BRACKETS. SAWED WORK

CAP AT A.

BRACKET.

G.E.HARNEY ARCHITECT 149 B'WAY. N.Y.

SECTION.

GABLE ON BRACKETS. SAWED AND CHAMPFERED WORK.

BRACKET.

PLAIN VERANDA. END.

SECTION.

FRONT.

VERANDA. SAWED AND CHAMPFERED WORK. END.

FRONT.

G.E. Harney, BICKNELL'S WOODEN & BRICK BUILDINGS, 1875

Building Details

WOODEN CORNICES.

ELEVATION.   SECTION.   ELEVATION.   SECTION.

BRACKET.   BRACKET.

RAFTERS and SCROLLS.

RAILINGS.

A.J. Bicknell, WOODEN & BRICK BUILDINGS, 1875

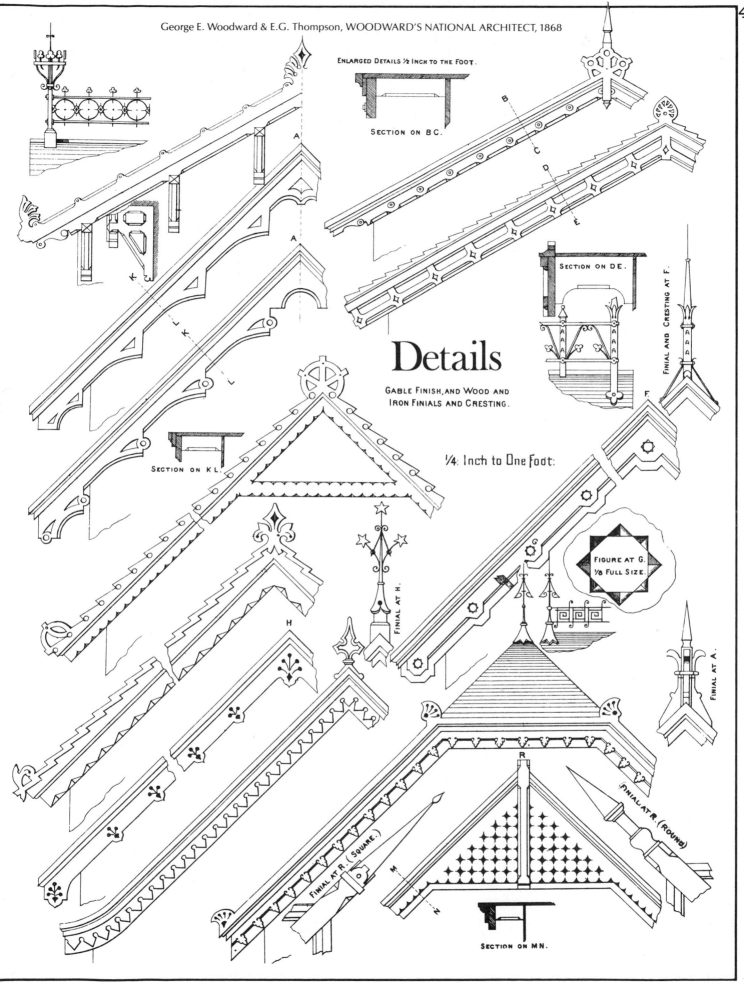

George E. Woodward & E.G. Thompson, WOODWARD'S NATIONAL ARCHITECT, 1868

ENLARGED DETAILS ½ INCH TO THE FOOT.

SECTION ON B C.

SECTION ON D E.

Details

GABLE FINISH, AND WOOD AND
IRON FINIALS AND CRESTING.

¼ Inch to One Foot.

SECTION ON K L.

FINIAL AND CRESTING AT F.

FIGURE AT G.
⅛ FULL SIZE.

FINIAL AT H.

FINIAL AT A.

FINIAL AT R. (ROUND)

FINIAL AT R. (SQUARE.)

SECTION ON M N.

Out~Building Details

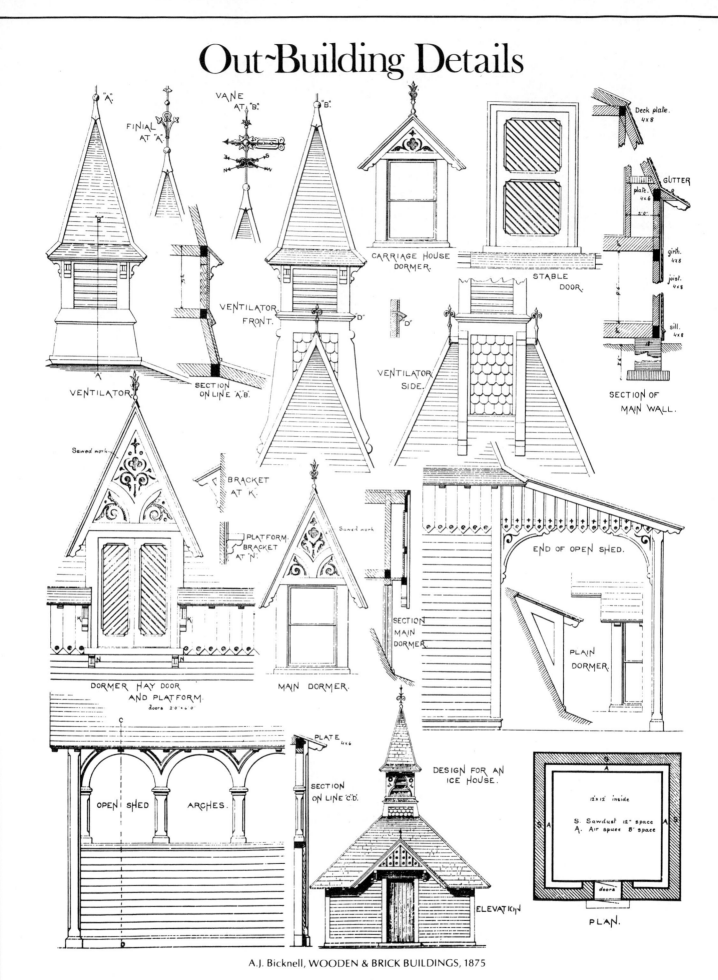

FINIAL AT "A".

VANE AT "B".

"B".

CARRIAGE HOUSE DORMER.

STABLE DOOR.

Deck plate. 4 x 8

GUTTER

plate. 4 x 6

girth. 4 x 8

joist. 4 x 8

sill. 4 x 8

VENTILATOR FRONT.

SECTION ON LINE A B.

"D"

VENTILATOR SIDE.

SECTION OF MAIN WALL.

VENTILATOR.

Sawed work.

BRACKET AT K.

PLATFORM BRACKET AT N.

Sawed work.

SECTION MAIN DORMER.

END OF OPEN SHED.

PLAIN DORMER.

DORMER HAY DOOR AND PLATFORM.
doors 2 0 x 6 0

MAIN DORMER.

PLATE 4 x 6

SECTION ON LINE C D.

DESIGN FOR AN ICE HOUSE.

OPEN SHED ARCHES.

ELEVATION

12 x 12 inside

S. Sawdust 12" space
A. Air space 8" space

PLAN.

A.J. Bicknell, WOODEN & BRICK BUILDINGS, 1875

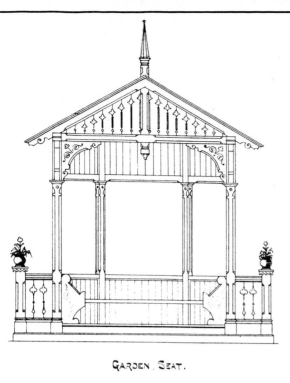

GARDEN. SEAT.

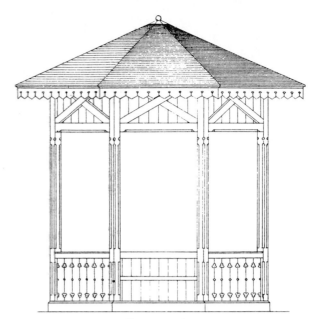

SUMMER. HOUSE.

Garden Improvements

A.J. Bicknell, WOODEN & BRICK BUILDINGS, 1875

WELL HOUSE.

OUT. HOUSE.

ICE HOUSE.

SCALE TO ELEVATIONS. — PLANS ONE HALF.

Cottage Gardening

I'll relate an incident connected with cottage gardening that may interest if it does not benefit some of those into whose hands this book may fall. About a dozen years ago I had the pleasure of making the acquaintance of a gentleman whose duties compelled him to be at his desk in a close office in the City of New York, from 9 o'clock A. M. to 4 P. M. Being naturally of a weak constitution, his sedentary life soon made him the victim of dyspepsia to such a degree that he felt that he must soon resign his situation. He was then a man of forty, entirely ignorant of anything pertaining to country life, and it was with great misgivings and reluctance that, by the advice of his physician, he changed his home from a closely built part of New York to a cottage in the then country-like suburb of Bergen Heights, N. J. His means enabled him to purchase a modest cottage built on a lot 50 by 150 feet ; he did not want the land, he said, but the cottage was such as he fancied, and the ground had to go with it. It was about this time that I formed his acquaintance, through some business transaction, and he asked my professional advice as to what he could do with his land, which he had already begun to consider somewhat of an incumbrance. I replied to him that, if I was not greatly mistaken, in his little plot of ground lay a cure for all his bodily ills, and that besides it could add to the comforts if not the luxuries of his table if he would only work it. "I work it !" he exclaimed. "You don't suppose that these hands could dig or delve," holding up his thin and bloodless fingers, "and if they could I know nothing about gardening." I told him I thought neither objection insurmountable if he once begun.

The result of our conversation was, that he resolved to try, and try he did to a purpose. Our interview was in March, and before the end of April he had his lot all nicely dug over, the labor being done by his own hands during an hour and a half each morning. His custom was to get up at six o'clock and work at his garden until half past seven. This gave him ample time to dress, get breakfast, and be at his desk in the city by nine. The labor of merely digging was (to him) heavy and rather monotonous, but he stuck to it bravely, and when he again presented himself before me for plants and seeds and information as to what to do with them, it was with some pride that I saw my prescription had worked so well, for my friend then looked more like a farmer than a pallid clerk. The regulating of his little garden was a simple matter, and was done according to the following diagram :

Cauliflower, cabbage and lettuce.	Strawberries.
Cucumbers, onions, and parsley.	Raspberries.
Beets, carrots, and parsnips.	Tomatoes.
Bush beans.	Asparagus and Rhubarb.

During his first season, of course, he made some blunders and some failures, but his interest in the work increased year by year. His family was supplied with an abundance of all the fresh vegetables and fruits his limited space could admit of being grown—a supply that it would have taken at least $150 to purchase at retail, and stale at that. But the benefit derived from the cultivation of this cottage garden was health—strong, rugged health—that for the six years he was my neighbor, never once failed him.

I know this case is an extremely exceptional one, for I never knew another man who so resolutely worked himself into health. There are hundreds of business men, book-keepers, salesmen, clerks, and the like who live in the suburbs of all great cities, many of whom can ill afford to pay for the keeping of the plots surrounding their cottages, but who think they can far less afford to do the work themselves. As a consequence, in nine cases out of ten, the rear, at least, of their suburban plots is a wilderness of weeds. But this is not the least of the evils, the owner has a certain amount of muscular force, and this, be it more or less, being unused, its possessor pays the penalty of his laziness in dyspepsia, and a host of other ills. The proofs are apparent everywhere that garden operations are conducive to health and longevity. The work is not unduly laborious, and when fairly entered into has a never-failing interest. The growing and the watching of the great variety of plants gives a healthy tone to the mind, while the physical labor demanded by cultivation takes care of the body.

Peter Henderson, GARDENING FOR PLEASURE, 1875

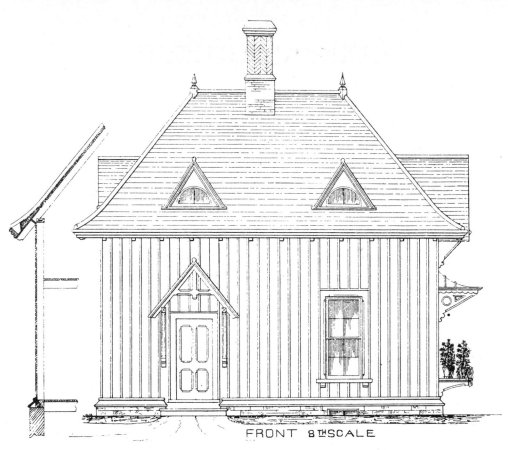

FRONT 8TH SCALE

William T. Hanlett, BICKNELL'S WOODEN & BRICK BUILDINGS, 1875

Gardener's Cottage

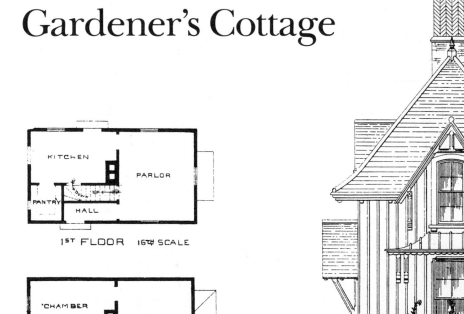

KITCHEN

PARLOR

PANTRY

DOWN UP

HALL

1ST FLOOR 16TH SCALE

'CHAMBER

CHAMBER

C. C.

DOWN

C.

HALL

2ND FLOOR

END

Cottage Furniture

Fig. 1.

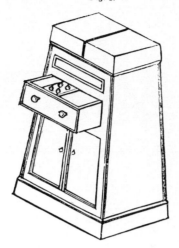

Fig. 2.

Fig. 1—Is a very convenient washstand, in high favor with the ladies. When not in use, the basin is concealed by two box covers, which are hinged, and which open and turn over when the stand is used, affording space for soap-holders, brush, trays, &c. There is a drawer below, with partitions for keeping these and various other articles belonging to the toilette; one partition having a flat board raised two inches from the bottom of the drawer, and being pierced with holes for perfume bottles, &c. Below this drawer there is a deep cupboard with double doors.

Fig. 2—Is a table for invalids, commonly called a bed-table, which is a very great convenience in sickness. The top of this table is made to rise or fall at pleasure, by raising or lowering the upper part of the pillar *a*, which is perforated with holes at given distances, to admit the peg *c*, and which works in a square groove in the centre of the lower part.

Fig. 3.

Fig. 4.

Fig. 3. A strong chair put together with mortice and tenon.

Fig. 4. A comfortable easy chair, with stuffed sides and bottom, movable cushions and castors.

Fig. 5.

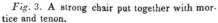

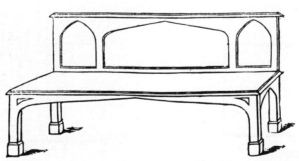

Fig. 5. Is a Gothic bench without arms or drawers, but with a paneled back and square legs.

Cottage Furniture

Fig. 1.

Fig. 2.

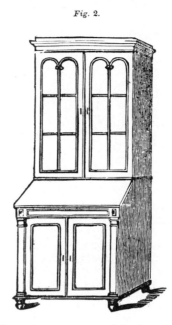

Fig. 1. Is a fixed corner cupboard in the Gothic style, with glazed doors.

Fig. 2. Is a secretary and book-case, with a
falling board, which serves as a writing-desk.

Fig. 3.

Fig. 3. Is a settle with drawers, often used in taverns. The back protects the sitter from the
current of air from the door.

Fig. 4.

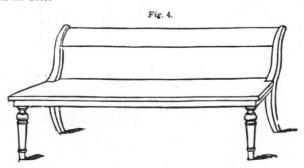

Fig. 4. Is a handsome Grecian bench, with turned legs.

Cottage Furniture

Fig. 1.

Fig. 2.

Fig. 3.

Fig. 1. Is a small tea or work-table. The top is hinged on a triangular box, which may be used to hold work in. When not in use, the top is set up on edge, and when brought down it fastens with a common catch fastening.

Fig. 2. Is a neat work-table, which may be made by any joiner out of the common woods of the country, at a very trifling expense.

Fig. 3. Is a small dressing-table with a drawer in front, to hold combs, brushes, &c.

Fig. 4.

Fig. 5.

Fig. 4. Is a circular flower-stand.

Fig. 5. Is a small wash hand-stand or table, in the Gothic style, with drawer, shelf, &c.

Fig. 6.

Fig. 7.

Fig. 6. Is a box footstool. The top is an outside frame, with webbing stretched across to support the stuffing above, which is covered with carpeting of the same kind as that of the floor of the room in which it is to be used. The sides are of wood, painted to match the other furniture.

Fig. 7. Is an extension table, with two folding leaves and two portable legs, unscrewed and taken off when the leaves are folded up.

Cottage Furniture

GODEY'S LADY'S BOOK, 1849

Fig. 1.

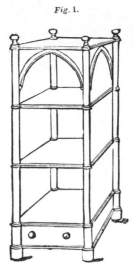

Fig. 2.

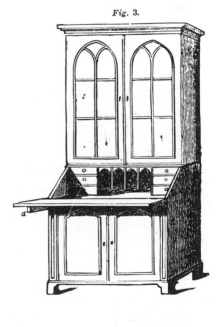

Fig. 3.

Fig. 1. A corner cupboard for glasses or china. It may also serve for a book-shelf, and the drawer for music or manuscripts.

Fig. 2. A plain wardrobe.
Fig. 3. A bureau book-case in the Gothic style.

KITCHEN SETTEE TABLE.
Gervase Wheeler, RURAL HOMES, 1851

A Farm House

We present this design with some confidence that it will be found to meet the wants of a large class of farmers and other dwellers in the country. It is neither large nor costly. It has neither a pretentious nor a foreign aspect. It seems as if it might have grown out of the soil itself, so modestly does it harmonize with the best features of any cultivated landscape. Yet it is roomy enough for quite a large family, and every room is arranged for home, family enjoyment, rather than for show or for company. Any family which will adapt itself to the suggestions

Fig. **1**—Principal Floor.

Fig. **2**—Chamber Plan.

of refinement and intelligence indicated by the green-house, the bay window and its crowning balcony, the latticed porch and the simple terrace, need never want more exciting pleasures than those always at command beneath and around the old roof-tree.

The accommodation provided is an entrance hall, a parlor of fair proportions, with a bay window, a glass door through which the plants in the green-house may be seen, and an alcove, which is a small recess cut off the veranda, and only separated from the parlor by an arch, and, if preferred, a fall of drapery. On its left wall a case of books, or articles of curiosity or *vertu*, may be placed; through its farther wall a glass door leads upon a small private veranda, enclosed by a light balustrade; and at the right, a private door gives a "favored few" access to the bed-room. The dining-room with its closet, the kitchen, the back stairs and the pantry, conclude the accommodation given on the first floor, (fig. **1**.) Everything in the way of a scullery, dairy, wood-room, &c., can of course be added according to the necessities of each particular case. Four good chambers (fig. **2**) are supplied in the attic, each with a closet.

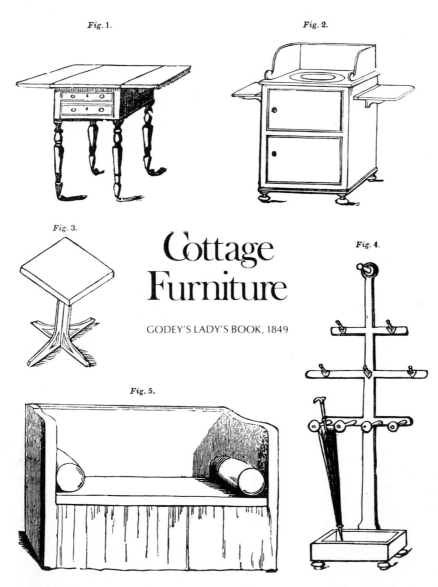

Fig. 1.

Fig. 2.

Fig. 3.

Cottage Furniture

GODEY'S LADY'S BOOK, 1849

Fig. 4.

Fig. 5.

Fig. 1.—A plain, parlor work table, with two drawers.

Fig. 2.—A wash-hand stand, enclosed, with two cupboards.

Fig. 3.—A stool.

Fig. 4.—A hat stand, with trough for umbrellas.

Fig. 5.—A sofa, with arrangement for being converted into a bed.

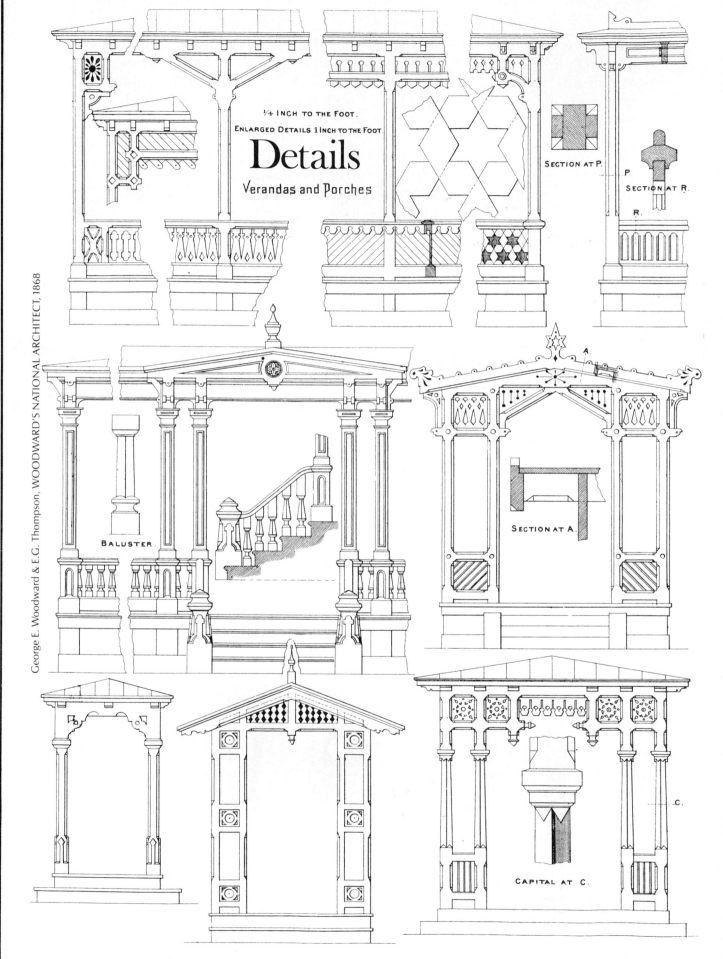

¼ INCH TO THE FOOT.

ENLARGED DETAILS 1 INCH TO THE FOOT.

Details

Verandas and Porches

SECTION AT P.

SECTION AT R.

BALUSTER.

SECTION AT A

CAPITAL AT C.

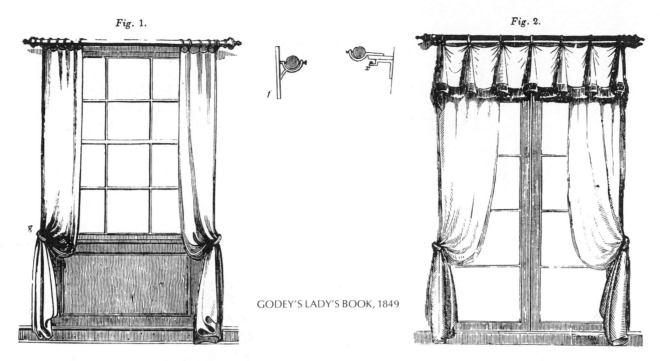

Fig. 1. *Fig.* 2.

GODEY'S LADY'S BOOK, 1849

Fig. 1 is a very plain style of curtains, hanging on a round pole supported at each end by a bracket, of which *f* is a section. The rings running on the pole are of brass or iron, gilt or bronzed.

Fig. 2 is a cottage window curtain in the Grecian style. The bracket, of which *r* is a sectional view, is of brass, screwed to a lath.

Curtains For Country Houses

Curtains.—Large double windows, or those that open lengthwise like a door, are difficult to fit with lambrequins and curtains ; but a light wire or cane frame projecting from over the window, deep enough to permit the blinds and windows to swing clear, can be fastened above the window, and both lambrequin and curtain suspended from that with very good effect. There is nothing more refreshing than plain white Swiss muslin curtains, open in the middle, looped back on either side with a broad band of insertion, over blue, green, or cherry ribbon. Or a strip of well-glazed paper muslin looks as well as ribbon, is much less expensive, and can be purchased in almost all of the delicate colors. Or the curtain may be simply tied back with ribbon. There should be a broad hem on each curtain, with ribbon or paper muslin laid inside the hem. By joining the hem to the curtain with a handsome insertion, and sewing a ruffle on the outer edge of the broad hem neatly fluted, one secures a charming effect from the parlor curtains. Lace curtains are very elegant, but difficult to do up so as to look like new, and somewhat expensive if one hire them cleaned by a French cleaner ; and are no more beautiful than these Swiss curtains, which can be easily cleaned, and fluted, and look new each time.

Lambrequins, made also of white Swiss to match the curtains, produce a very airy, cheerful effect, or the lambrequins can be made of damask, or cretonne, with its rich, soft colors, and trimmed with heavy fringe. If one has not confidence in one's own skill to cut and shape these lambrequins, any upholsterer will shape them, and then it is easy work to trim and put them up.

Mrs. H. Beecher, ALL AROUND THE HOUSE, 1879

A Small Rural Double Cottage

A SMALL RURAL DOUBLE COTTAGE. - for two small families. Under the farmer's living-room is a basement-kitchen, with the windows considerably out of ground, and under the coachman's kitchen is a cellar: the entrances are, as will be perceived, quite distinct. Up stairs the farmer has three bedrooms; the coachman but one, according to instructions. Such a cottage would cost about $1800, neatly finished.

Such a plan would not be unsuitable for a lodge, in which the families of a gardener and gate-keeper could live, or it might be fitted up a little more completely, and offer convenient accommodation to two friends who felt inclined to build it on some agreeable rural lot for a few months' quiet residence in the summer.

It seems strange that this idea should not be more frequently acted on than is the case at present. Far away from the fashionable watering-places, but easily accessible from the cities—in the heart of Vermont, for instance—may be found bold, beautiful scenery, pure air, and a pleasant neighborhood. Land is cheap, timber cheap, living cheap, and all of the best. These are the spots that should attract the attention of heads of families who wish to give their young people the benefit of country life in the summer.

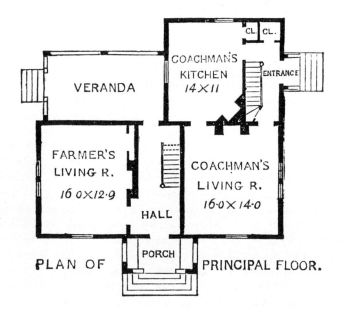

PLAN OF PRINCIPAL FLOOR.

Calvert Vaux, VILLAS AND COTTAGES, 1857

Cottage in the Rural Gothic Style

WHILE we have endeavored to concentrate within moderate limits the necessary conveniences of a comfortable mode of living for the occupants, we have not neglected the outward expression of taste that contributes so largely to the pleasure of the beholder. A plain building, by a few, simple, well-directed touches, can thus be invested with a character approaching the ornate. A brief analysis of the design before us will attest the truth of the above remark. Remove first the barge and eave treatment, and we destroy at once the *polish* of the expression; but take away the pinnacles, and we greatly weaken the expression itself, almost entirely depriving it of that piquancy that strikes us so forcibly in the present view. The analysis might be pushed further, to the consideration of the effect of removing dormers, changing the style of chimney tops, etc.; but we have said enough to show what

" Great effects from little causes flow."

ACCOMMODATION.—The internal arrangements of this dwelling are so plainly exhibited on the plan of principal floor, fig. 1 , as scarcely to need explanation. G is an open entrance porch. A, 8 by 16 feet, is the entrance hall, and contains a flight of stairs. B, 16 by 18 feet, is the dining-room, lighted by a recessed twin window, and having an ample china closet attached. The parlor C, 16 by 16 feet, has a nice bay-window, but would be improved by a window extending to the floor on the side next to the entrance porch, an idea not fully conveyed by the engraving. The kitchen D, 16 by 16 feet, is well lighted, and provided with sink, side entrance, and small closet. Adjoining the kitchen there is a wash-house, 11 by 12 feet, and beyond this a wood-house or pump-room F, 7 by 12 feet, having outdoor communication independent of the kitchen.

Ascending to the second floor, fig. 2 we find the stair landing, marked by the letter H, from which we have ready access to the chambers I and J, and to the bed-room K and bath-room L. The chambers, as will be seen, are all furnished with good closets.

CONSTRUCTION.—A very pretty effect would be secured by building this cottage of wood, the weatherboarding being put on in the vertical manner, and the joints battened after one of the methods explained at fig. 8. The gable and eave cornice should be cut from 3-inch plank, in a bold manner, and also the ornament against the base of the pinnacles.

ESTIMATE.—Built of wood, in the manner above described, the cost of this design would not vary much from $4000, where timber is plenty; built of stone, and the walls furred inside for plastering, $650 should be added.

Samuel Sloan, HOMESTEAD ARCHITECTURE, 1861

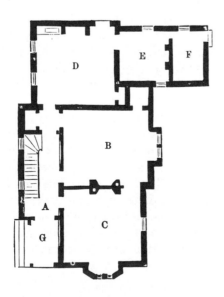

1 —PRINCIPAL FLOOR.

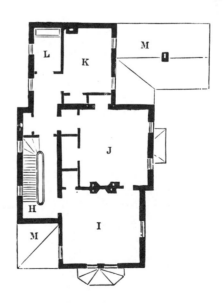

2 —SECOND FLOOR.

An Artist's Studio & Cottage

The vignette illustrates an artist's studio, designed for Mr. Jervis M'Entee, landscape painter, of Rondout, and built by him of wood, fitted in a substantial, simple way, for $400. It is finely placed on an elevated site, and commands an extended view of the Kaatskills and the Hudson. On the plan it is one simple room: the ceiling line follows the line of the roof and collar beams, so as to give height and a more airy effect to the interior. All the rafters are left visible, the plastering being fitted between them. Some time after the design had been built and occupied, Mr. M'Entee added a portion of a simple cottage residence in corresponding style, the studio still remaining in use for its original purpose. The complete effect aimed at is shown on the lower view and plan.

As the parlor, the veranda, and the porch are not yet built, a somewhat disproportioned result is obtained *for the present*, as the wing looks larger than the house; but its accommodation and cost, as it stands, is all sufficient for the immediate needs and circumstances of its proprietor, who has judiciously preferred to run the gauntlet of his neighbors' criticism for a time, and to plan his house as he *will* want it, carrying it out by degrees as opportunity offers, rather than to adopt a snug arrangement complete in itself, which, although suitable enough for to-day, would, in all probability, be in a few years inconveniently small for his own needs; and if he wanted to sell at any time, could hardly fail to prove an undesirable investment on a site constantly improving in value, and that might, in all probability, be disposed of to advantage at any time, with a roomy house on it, or a building that could easily be made a good family residence, without pulling down the existing building or injuring its general appearance. The house as it at present stands, with hall, dining-room, pantry, small bedroom, and studio, on principal floor, three bedrooms and a little bath-room above, and basement kitchen, with cellars below, has cost $2000; and Mr. M'Entee calculates that another $1000 would render it complete, as shown, giving a second kitchen below, a best parlor and a best bedroom over, in addition to the accommodation already provided.

DESIGN FOR AN ARTIST'S STUDIO.

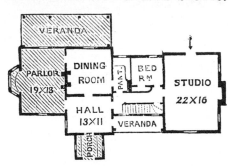

PLAN OF PRINCIPAL FLOOR.

N.E.VIEW.

SHOWING THE COTTAGE COMPLETED.

Calvert Vaux, VILLAS AND COTTAGES, 1857

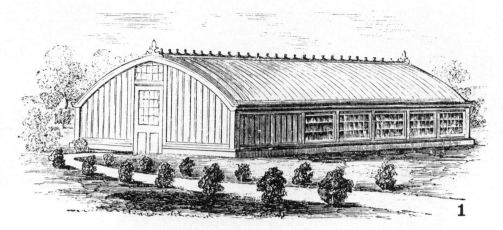

George E. & F.W. Woodward, GRAPERIES AND HORTICULTURAL BUILDINGS, 1865

Green House

Fig. 1 is a perspective view of the house. The west end is boarded and battened. This corresponds with the general design of the house, and presents a neat finish. The sides, except the potting room, are of glass, the sashes being about three feet high. Every other sash is hung at the bottom, for the purpose of ventilation. The roof is a continuous glazed roof, and is quite flat, which is a decided advantage to the plants within. There are no ventilators in the roof, the top ventilation being effected by means of the sashes over the doors at each end, which are hung at the bottom for this purpose, and afford abundant ventilation for a house the length of this one. There is an ornamental crest along the ridge, and at each end a neat finial.

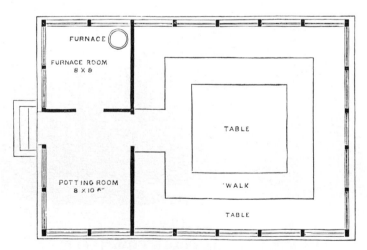

2 –*Ground Plan.*

PEALE'S POPULAR EDUCATOR, 1883

A Rural Cottage

The accompanying plan of a rural cottage was awarded a premium which was offered some few years ago. The outside appearance is attractive, light and pleasant, and is not over-ornamental, a great fault with many modern houses. The rooms are large and most conveniently arranged, every room of the ground floor being pleasant enough for a parlor or a living-room.

inches by 14 feet 6 in. ; *Library*, 15 feet by 14 feet 6 inches ; *Kitchen*, 12 feet 6 inches by 13 feet 6 inches ; *Wash-Room*, 12 feet by 8 feet ; *Hall*, 6 feet 5 inches in width.

SECOND STORY. *A*, bed-room, 14 feet 5 inches by 11 feet 9 inches ; *B*, chamber, 18 feet 9 inches by 15 feet ; *C, C*, halls ; *D*, bed-room, 9 feet 6 inches by 11 feet ; *E*, bed-room, 14 feet 6 inches

GROUND PLAN.

D. R., dining-room, 18 feet 9 inches by 15 feet; *Parlor*, 18 feet 9 by 11 feet; *F*, servants' bed-room, 12 feet 6 inches by 14 feet 6 inches ; *G*, passage, 3 feet 6 inches in width.

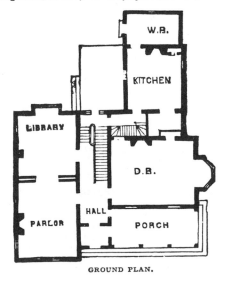

GROUND PLAN.

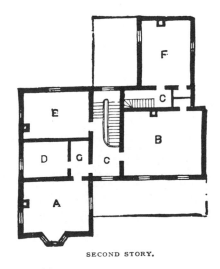

SECOND STORY.

Trees

J.J. Thomas, REGISTER OF RURAL AFFAIRS, 1860

THE BALDNESS OF NEW PLACES.—The remorseless manner in which the native trees have been totally cleared away from country residences, has left most of them in a very bleak and unsheltered situation. A neighbor had a fine natural oak grove before his house, but being strongly imbued with the cut-and-slash mania, chopped them all down, and then planted a row of maples in their place, which would require about thirty years to attain the size of the oaks. Sir Joshua Reynolds said he would paint Folly in the shape of a boy climbing over a high fence with an open gate close at his side. He might have done it more effectually by representing an American land-owner cutting down all his native shade trees, that he might enjoy transplanted ones thirty years afterwards.

There are, however, many places where a thin natural growth of trees may be found, and among which a residence may be built. Yet with a most singular fatuity, such land-owners avoid these beautiful natural parks, and build in an open field adjacent. We witness frequent instances of this folly.

Where trees have grown up thinly, their heads have become rounded and well developed, and nothing is easier than to remove those possessing the least beauty, or which may stand in the range of fine landscape views. Even such as have grown closely together, and have shot up bare trunks, may be greatly improved in appearance in a few years, by heading them down soon after thinning out, as low as a good supply of side branches will admit, and gradually bringing them down into a fine form in successive years. The addition of other trees by planting, will soon greatly improve the appearance of the whole, and impart to the wildness and crudeness of nature, the grace and finish of an embellished landscape.

Where necessity leads to the selection of such places as have no trees, the most rapid mode of supplying the deficiency is, first to prepare the soil in the best manner by trenching or deep subsoiling, at the same time working in large quantities of old manure or compost. Then plant moderate-sized, thrifty trees, which have been carefully taken up, and keep the soil bare and mellow for a few years, foregoing the pleasure of a green turf for the sake of a more rapid growth of the trees. Large trees when set out present a more conspicuous appearance at first, and some may be interspersed, but in a short period the smaller ones will have outstripped them, and will then present a richer, more dense, and far more beautiful foliage. By selecting a portion of the most rapidly-growing sorts, as the Silver Maple, the European Larch, and the Abele, among deciduous trees; and the Norway Spruce, Scotch Pine and Austrian Pine, among evergreens, a more speedy effect will be secured.

H.W. Cleveland, William & Samuel D. Backus, VILLAGE AND FARM COTTAGES, 1856

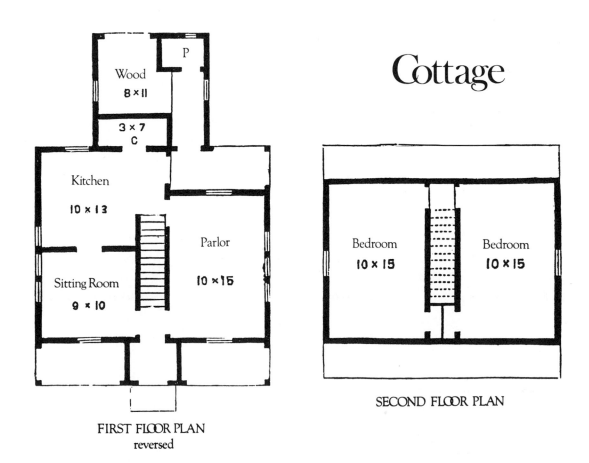

Cottage

FIRST FLOOR PLAN
reversed

SECOND FLOOR PLAN

Cottage

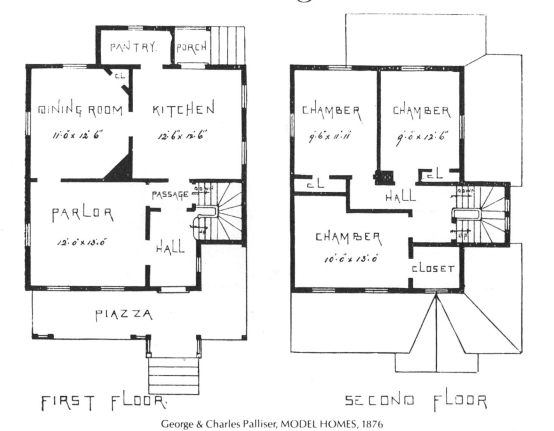

PANTRY. PORCH

DINING ROOM
11'-0" x 12'-6"

KITCHEN
12'-6" x 12'-6"

CL

PARLOR
12'-0" x 13'-0"

PASSAGE

HALL

PIAZZA

FIRST FLOOR.

CHAMBER
9'-6" x 11'-11"

CHAMBER
9'-0" x 12'-6"

CL HALL CL

CHAMBER
10'-0" x 13'-0"

CLOSET

SECOND FLOOR

George & Charles Palliser, MODEL HOMES, 1876

George E. & F.W. Woodward, COUNTRY HOMES, 1865

Stable

This stable may be constructed either of wood, or of stone. It contains stalls for four horses, and affords space for their accomodation, together with a harness room and a tool closet. This latter is a convenience very essential to the comfort of the owner, as well as to the proper care and preservation of such implements as belong especially to the carriage house and stable.

This building should be surrounded and screened with fruit trees and shrubbery, and then, with its evident architectural effects, it will become an attractive feature in the landscape of which it becomes a part, with the other accessories of the elegant country home.

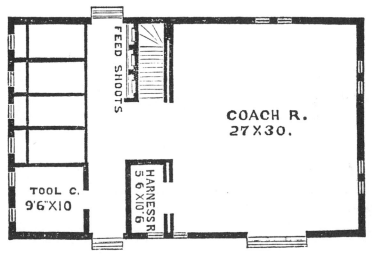

FEED SHOOTS

COACH R.
27X30.

HARNESS R.
5 6 X 10.6

TOOL C.
9'6"X10

Plan

Stable

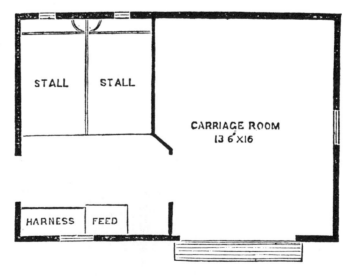

Plan
(*Reversed.*)

George E. & F.W. Woodward, COUNTRY HOMES, 1865

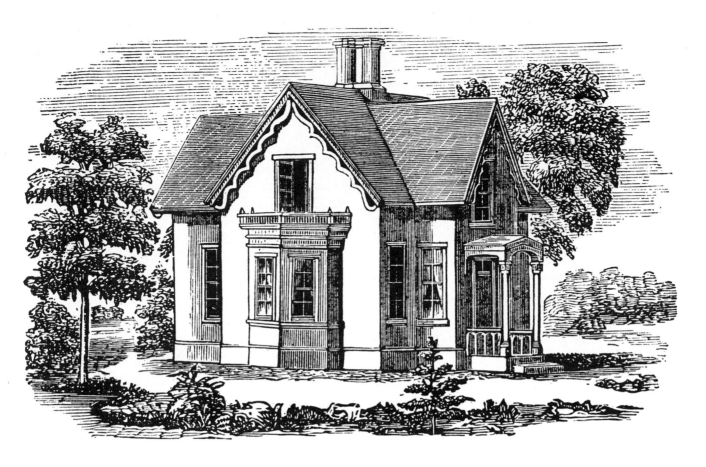

A Semi~Southern Cottage

This is a house well adapted to the Middle and Southern States, although for the latter a veranda should be thrown around the front and sides.

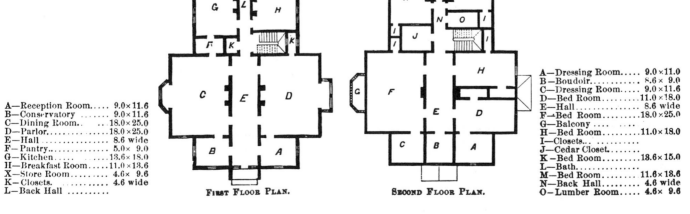

FIRST FLOOR PLAN.

SECOND FLOOR PLAN.

A—Reception Room..... 9.0 × 11.6
B—Conservatory .... 9.0 × 11.6
C—Dining Room.. ...18.0 × 25.0
D—Parlor............18.0 × 25.0
E—Hall .... 8.6 wide
F—Pantry.............. 5.0 × 9.0
G—Kitchen..... ....13.6 × 18.0
H—Breakfast Room.....11.0 × 13.6
X—Store Room........ 4.6 × 9.6
K—Closets. ....4.6 wide
L—Back Hall ....

A—Dressing Room..... 9.0 × 11.0
B—Boudoir.......... 8.6 × 9.0
C—Dressing Room..... 9.0 × 11.6
D—Bed Room.........11.0 × 18.0
E—Hall .... 8.6 wide
F—Bed Room.........18.0 × 25.0
G—Balcony ....
H—Bed Room.........11.0 × 18.0
I—Closets.. ....
J—Cedar Closet.......
K—Bed Room.........18.6 × 15.0
L—Bath..............
M—Bed Room........11.6 × 18.6
N—Back Hall .... 4.6 wide
O—Lumber Room..... 4.6 × 9.6

D.H. Jacques, THE HOUSE, 1859

A Picturesque Stone Cottage

BEAUTY of outline and proportion is as important in the design and construction of a house, as the interior arrangement of the dwelling. A "square box' may afford all necessary facilities to the family, but if it does not please the eye and gratify the esthetic as well as the animal wants, it lacks an indispensable part of what a fine country house ought to be. The large number of houses which have been put up during the last three or four years on the great thoroughfares of travel leading out of New York, have afforded a good opportunity for the exercise of the talents of our Architects, and the skill of our suburban Builders. The design we give (No. 1) was executed of stone, at "Highwood Park," Tenafly Station, on the line of the Northern New Jersey Rail Road, and situate on the western Palisade slope.

Fig. 1, is a perspective view, and Figs. 2 and 3 are first and second floor plans. The style is a modification of the Gothic, with "bell-cast" roof. The main building is 17 x 30 feet, and the extension 20 x 21 feet. The whole, two stories and attic, with a cellar and a basement kitchen below. Exposure, south-westerly. The first floor, Fig. 2, contains: L, lobby, 5 x 8 feet; P, parlor, 13½ x 14 feet; D, dining-room, 14 x 17½ feet; H, open hall and staircase; K, kitchen, 13 x 14 feet, besides sink-room, pantry and china-closet. Fig. 3, is the second floor plan, containing three sleeping rooms, 13 x 14 feet; a bath-room, 6 x 10 feet, with a passage for communication from front to rear rooms, and wardrobe at the side; c, c, are closets. The attic contains space for four rooms, about 8 x 10 and 12 feet. The parlor and dining room are separated by folding doors, and may be *en suite* when required; and are warmed, with the chambers above them, by the furnace.

Cost.—The cost of the house, including a well, entrance gates, grading and walks, will not exceed $6,000. The following are the principal items of cost. The walls, the most costly item, were laid up in random courses of silicious, or sand stone, white and red, and contain about—

5,000 cubic feet of stone work at 30c., ...	$1,500 00
(This includes pointing and excavation for cellar.)	
8,000 feet timber and rough lumber at 24-00, ...	192 00
Shingles, lath, flooring, finishing pine, architraves and moulds, &c., cartage and freight, ...	850 00
Sashes, doors and blinds, ...	368 00
Lathing and plastering, cistern and chimneys, ...	375 00
Carpenter work, about 275 days, at $3, ...	825 00
Painting, ...	250 00
Plumbing, (pump, sink and piping), ...	80 00
Furnace and setting, ...	250 00
Hardware, about, ...	200 00
Lightning conductors, ...	68 00
Speaking tubes, ...	15 00
The wells walks, grading and gates, ...	700 00

Daniel T. Atwood, COUNTRY & SUBURBAN HOUSES, 1871

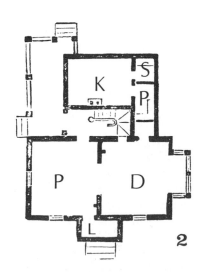

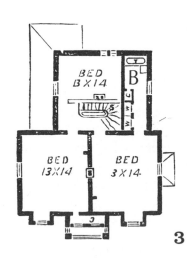

Samuel Sloan, HOMESTEAD ARCHITECTURE, 1861

We mean what we say when we pay this design the high compliment of calling it American, and we think our readers will sustain us in the application of the very comprehensive term. Simple in form, convenient and economical in arrangement, tasteful yet unassuming in detail, we know of no title so expressive of its deserts as the one we have given it. Although it possesses no trait preventive of its recognition as an important country residence in any part of the Union, we conceive that it would be a decidedly acceptable dwelling to the well-to-do resident of the Western prairie. The umbrage afforded the windows by the canopies and balconies, while enhancing the boldness of the design, contributes greatly to the comfort of the apartments by protecting the glass from the noonday summer sun, even in the Northern and Western States.

CONSTRUCTION.—The great abundance of wood in some portions of our country, the facility with which it is transported from a timber region to a prairie, and the ease with which it is adapted to building, will be reason enough for using it for that purpose for generations to come. The design before us is intended to be constructed of wood.

ESTIMATE.—An excellent and substantial house may be built after this plan for $3700, in any part of Pennsylvania,—the stories being 10 and 9 feet in the clear respectively; the exterior painted a warm, drab color, slightly tinged with blue, and the roof covered with white pine shingles, about 5 inches or one-third their length to the weather.

A Bracketed American Cottage

ACCOMMODATION.—From the front piazza F, fig. 1. the passage of 6 feet wide is entered, which gives access to all the rooms; an outside entrance is also given in the end of the building through the stair hall. A, 16 by 20 feet, is designed for a parlor; B, 16 by 16 feet, is a sitting-room; C, 16 by 20 feet, a dining-room; D, 16 by 16 feet, a kitchen; and E, a pantry, affording also a passage from dining-room to kitchen. We may remark here, that a veranda extending the full length of parlor and dining-room would be a very beneficial addition to this design, both for use and appearance. In accordance with the apparent demand for such an improvement, we have shown it in the perspective.

A Rural Gothic Farm-House

PEALE'S POPULAR EDUCATOR, 1883

In this plan for a rural home, with the exception of the cornice on the gables and a few cheap brackets, there is no ornamentation to cause an unnecessary outlay of money, and nothing likely to get out of repair, as is often the case with the flimsy ornaments attached to so many modern cottages.

This house is in the *Rural Gothic style,* a style which, with its broken outline, its verandas and bay windows, expresses no small amount of domestic and home feeling.

monotonous appearance of that side of the building, and balancing in a degree the mass of the other side.

The main roof rises at an angle of 45°; the wood-house part is one-story; roof, one-fourth pitch. The inside is finished appropriately, plain and neat. The lower story is nine feet high in the clear; the upper story, finished to collar-beams, is eight feet six inches. The cellar under kitchen and dining-room is well lighted, and

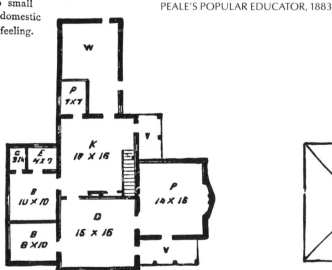

FIRST FLOOR.

P, Parlor; *D,* Dining-Room; *K,* Kitchen; *B, B,* Bed-Rooms; *C,* Closet; *E,* Bath; *P,* Pantry; *V, V,* Verandas; *W,* Wood-house.

The house was planned for a family who aim to do their own work; therefore utility, compactness and economy of labor were first considered. Yet the external appearance is quite picturesque and truthful. The part containing the two bed-rooms, bathing and clothes-room is quite economically obtained, it being a lean-to addition, one story high, with a flattish roof. Above this is a gabled window, with its stool resting on this roof. This gable rises to the height of the main roof, thus breaking the otherwise

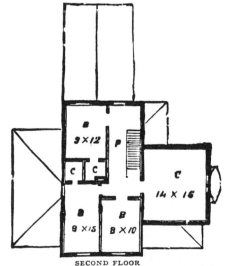

SECOND FLOOR

B, B, B, Bed-Rooms; *C,* Chamber; *c, c,* Closets; *P,* Passage.

the chimney, standing in the centre, is furnished with openings for ventilation. With this arrangement the cellar can be kept sweet and wholesome. The rooms are warmed by stoves. Fire-places may be easily built in the dining-room and kitchen, if desired. The bathing-room is easily accessible, it being connected with the kitchen bed-room, which renders it a convenient and useful apartment.

The cost of this house, with a light timber frame, clapboarded, lined on the inside with inch lumber, then furred with strip lath, lathed and plastered with two coats finish, is about $1,100.

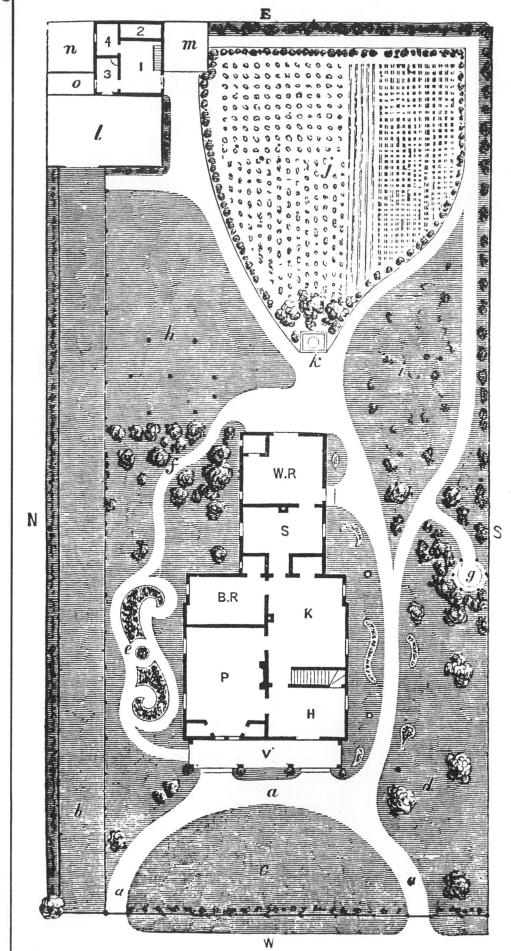

Stable

1, Tool room.

2, Poultry room.

3, Cow stall.

4, Feed room.

Yard

a, Walk.

b, Stable path.

c, Lawn.

d, Shrubbery.

e, Flower bed.

f, Evergreen screen.

h, Clothes yard.

i, Fruit.

j, Vegetables.

g. Summer house.

k, Well.

l, Cow yard.

m. Poultry yard.

n, Piggery.

o, Manure pit.

H.W. Cleveland, William & Samuel D. Backus, VILLAGE AND FARM COTTAGES, 1856

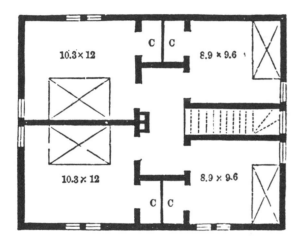

SECOND FLOOR PLAN.

10.3 × 12   C C   8.9 × 9.6

10.3 × 12   C C   8.9 × 9.6

Cottage

v, Verandah.

H, Hall.

P, Parlor.

K, Kitchen.

B R, Bedroom.

S, Scullery.

W R, Wood room.

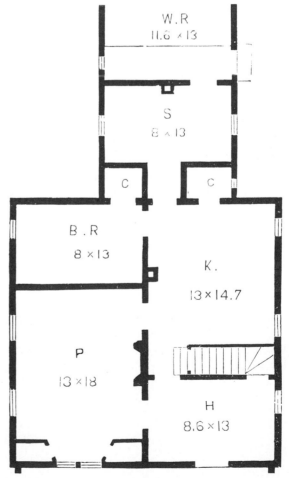

W.R
11.6 × 13

S
8 × 13

C   C

B.R
8 × 13

K.
13 × 14.7

P
13 × 18

H
8.6 × 13

FIRST STORY PLAN.

George E. Woodward & E.G. Thompson, WOODWARD'S NATIONAL ARCHITECT, 1868

Prices of Building Materials and Labor

At New York, January 1869

Estimates in this work are based on the prices here given, and cost of erection in other localities will be fixed by the local prices of materials.

MASON WORK AND MATERIALS.
Stone wall, including all materials, laid dry, per foot 23 cents.
do   do laid with mortar,   -   -   do   23   do.
Excavation, per cubic yard,   -   -   -   40   do.
Brick, per thousand, laid.   Pale, $19 50 to $23 50.   Hard burned, $21 to $25.
Cement, per barrel, $2 50 to $3.
Lime,   do $1 75.
Hair, per bushel,   70 cents.
Lath and plastering, including all materials, 1 coat, per square yard, 40 cents.
    do   do   do   2 coats,   do   60   do.
    do   do   do   3 coats,   do   70   do.
Laths, per thousand, $3 50 to $4 50.

Prices for all the timber, covering, flooring and finishing lumber, per thousand feet, board measure.

FRAMING TIMBER.
Pine, $45.   Sawed to order.   Spruce, $25.   Sawed to order.
Hemlock, $22 to $25.
Firring, 2 inches wide, 6 cents each.
Studding, 13 feet by 2×4 inches, 21 cents each. 3×4, 24 cents each.
Shingles, $8 to $10.

ROOFING.
Hemlock, 1 inch thick, $24 per thousand.
Pine, $1\frac{1}{4}$ inches thick, matched, $45 per thousand.
Spruce,   do   do $35   do
Slating, per square of 100 feet, metal extra.   1st quality of slates, $15.   2d quality, $14.
Tinning, per square of 100 feet, $11 to $13.
Leaders, 4 inches calibre, per lineal foot, 30 cents.

FLOORING.
Spruce, 5 inches wide, $1\frac{1}{4}$-inch thick, $35 per thousand, planed and matched.
Spruce, 10 inches wide, $1\frac{1}{4}$-inch thick, planed and matched, $35 per thousand,
White pine, 5 inches wide, as above, $45.
White pine, 10 inches wide, as above, $45.
Georgia pine, 3 to 5 inches wide, $60 to $80, $1\frac{1}{4}$-inch thick, planed and matched.
Hemlock, 1-inch thick, matched, $24.

FINISHING STOCK, SEASONED.
Clear white pine, $65 per thousand.
Second quality of clear pine, $40 to $50.

HARDWARE.
Nails, per cwt., $5 75.

LABOR PER DAY.
Stone Mason, $4 00.
Bricklayer,   5 00.
Plasterer,   5 50.

Mason's Tender, $3 00.
Carpenter,   3 75.
Painter,   3 50.

Laborer, $2 00.

Noteworthy Suggestions

Having introduced to the reader the specific plans, etc., which will guide him in the erection of a home, a few general words of advice and suggestion will be in order.

It will be well to remember that no architect allows himself, when planning a house, to be guided by any cast-iron set of rules.

A house is a good deal like a suit of clothes, of which a fair fit may be obtained at the ready-made store, while, if close-fitting and stylish garments are wanted, the man's measure is taken and the articles made to order. In the country care should be taken not to make the house too high. Ground is cheap, and a home in the country which spreads over a goodly extent of ground has a certain air of elbow-room and capacity about it that the most magnificent four-story city dwelling fails to possess.

When building projections, window sills, etc., take care to provide a "deep molding" underneath, so that rain-water will drip off. Otherwise it will gather up the dust upon them and run down the walls, leaving mouldy streaks behind.

Where there is no plumbing in the house, the best place for the bath-room is next to the kitchen. Have the range placed against the bath-room partition and place a large tin boiler on the back of the range. From the back of the boiler carry a faucet through the partition to open over a bath-tub. By this means the carrying of water to and fro is dispensed with. To discharge the water from the bath, run a small pipe to a distance of twenty feet from the house and let it end there in a large hole filled in with loose stones and covered with earth. The water when discharged into this hole will soak away into the ground and do no harm, as it is not polluted.

To avoid rats or fire spreading through a house it is advisable to put one course of bricks in mortar at each floor level in all the furrings and partitions.

For the finest effect of foliage use trees and shrubbery as a background and flanking for the principal building. Too many large trees in the foreground cut off the view; besides, they keep out the sunshine, prevent free atmospheric circulation, and injure the house by concentrating upon it dampness and shade.

When a low site for a dwelling cannot be avoided be careful to have a thorough system of under-draining. See that the cellar-wall is raised considerably above the ground and that enough soil is spread around the house to make a yard which will shed the water readily. In a case of this kind every sanitary advantage offered by sun, soil, shelter and prospect should be carefully improved.

A square house includes more space within a given length of wall than any rectangular shape.

Of the whole house the front, and of the front the main entrance, should show the most pains in the direction of ornamentation.

Care in the disposition of rooms will save thousands of steps to those who do the house-work. Kitchen and dining-room should always be adjoining apartments. The dining-room is the place for the china closet. A wood-shed connecting with the kitchen by a covered way is a great convenience in inclement weather.

A multiplicity of closets is an invaluable boon to the housewife.

Frame houses exclude the cold much better if the studding is covered with tongued and grooved sheathing, and this in turn by tarred paper, the weather-boarding being placed over the whole. The sheathing and weather-boarding should be fitted closely around door and window frames, and the tarred paper allowed to lap over a little where a crack is likely to occur.

Where ingrain carpets, usually a yard wide, are to be used, the economical cutting will be helped by having either the length or breadth of each room some multiple of the width, as fifteen feet, eighteen feet, etc.

The difference between slate-roofing and shingles is about two cents per square foot, and where the former is used the difference in outlay purchases practically everlasting durability, a fire-proof roof, and purer rain-water in the cistern.

If free from sap, shingles will last from twenty to thirty years.

An attic, running the full length of the house, with windows at both ends, will prove a fine drying-room in bad weather.

PEALE'S POPULAR EDUCATOR, 1883

H.W. Cleveland, William & Samuel D. Backus, VILLAGE AND FARM COTTAGES, 1856

SHOPPEL'S MODERN HOUSES/1887

MODERN AMERICAN DWELLINGS/1897

THE 1870 AGRICULTURIST